THE PRIEST, MINISTER OF DIVINE MERCY

AN AID FOR CONFESSORS AND SPIRITUAL DIRECTORS

CONGREGATION FOR THE CLERGY

All documents are published thanks to the generous support of the members of the Catholic Truth Society

CATHOLIC TRUTH SOCIETY
PUBLISHERS TO THE HOLY SEE

CONTENTS

Contents

II. THE MINISTRY OF SPIRITUAL DIRECTION AS AN EXERCISE OF PASTORAL CHARITY

PRESENTATION

"It is necessary to return to the confessional as a place in which to celebrate the Sacrament of Reconciliation, but also as a place in which "to dwell" more often, so that the faithful may find compassion, advice and comfort, feel that they are loved and understood by God and experience the presence of Divine Mercy beside the Real Presence in the Eucharist"[1]

With these words, the Holy Father Pope Benedict XVI addressed confessors during the recent Year for Priests, indicating to each one present the importance and therefore the apostolic urgency of rediscovering the Sacrament of Reconciliation, both from their viewpoint of penitents as well as that of ministers.

Along with the daily celebration of the Eucharist, the availability of the priest to hear sacramental confessions, to welcome penitents, and to accompany them spiritually when they so request, is the real measure of a priest's pastoral charity. By their availability, priests give joyful witness and in a certain sense take upon themselves their true identity, redefined in the Sacrament of Holy Orders and not reducible to a mere functionality.

The priest is a minister, which is to say that he is at the same time both a servant and a prudent dispenser of Divine Mercy. To him is entrusted the serious responsibility "to forgive or to retain sins" (cf. *John* 20: 23). Through him, and through the power of the Spirit who is the Lord and Giver of Life, the faithful are able to experience today in the Church the joy of the Prodigal Son, who after a life of sin returned to his father's house in the manner of a servant but was welcomed with the dignity of a son.

Whenever a confessor is available, sooner or later a penitent will arrive. And if the confessor continues to make himself available, even stubbornly so, sooner or later many penitents will arrive!

Our rediscovery of the Sacrament of Reconciliation, both as penitents and as ministers, is a measure of authentic faith in the saving action of God which shows itself more clearly in the power of grace than in human strategic or pastoral initiatives which sometimes overlook this essential truth.

---

[1] BENEDICT XVI, *Allocution to the participants in the Course on the Internal Forum organized by the Tribunal of the Apostolic Penitentiary*, 11 March 2010.

Responding to the appeal of the Holy Father and expressing his profound intent, this aid is intended as yet another fruit of the Year for Priests, to be a helpful instrument for the ongoing formation of the Clergy and an aid in rediscovering the indispensible value of the Sacrament of Reconciliation and of Spiritual Direction.

The new evangelization and the ongoing renewal of the Church, *semper reformanda*, draw their life blood from the true sanctification of each member of the Church. It is clear that sanctification must precede both evangelization and renewal, for it lays claim to and forms the necessary precondition for every effective apostolic effort, as well as for the reform of the Clergy.

In the generous celebration of the Sacrament of Divine Mercy, each priest is called to experience for himself the uniqueness and the indispensability of the ministry entrusted to him. Such an experience will help him to avoid the "ever-changing sense of identity" which so often marks the existence of some priests. Instead, his experience will cultivate within himself that sense of wonder which fills his heart, for through no merit of his own he is called by God, in the Church, to break the Eucharistic Bread and to forgive the sins of others.

With these thoughts, we entrust the distribution and the fruits of this aid to the Blessed Virgin Mary, Refuge of Sinners and Mother of Divine Grace.

Vatican City, 9 March 2011
Ash Wednesday

MAURO Card. PIACENZA
Prefect

✠ CELSO MORGA IRUZUBIETA
Titular Archbishop of Alba marittima
Secretary

INTRODUCTION: TOWARDS HOLINESS

1. "At all times and in every race God has given welcome to whosoever fears Him and does what is right.(85) God, however, does not make men holy and save them merely as individuals, without bond or link between one another. Rather has it pleased Him to bring men together as one people, a people which acknowledges Him in truth and serves Him in holiness"[2]. On the journey to holiness to which the Lord calls each one of us (cf. *Mt* 5: 48; *Eph* 1:4), God deigns that we come to the help of one another. In this way we become mediators in Christ, as it were, to draw others near to his eternal love. This is the horizon of charity in which the celebration of the Sacraments of Penance and the practice of Spiritual direction may be found, and it is they that constitute the object of the present document.

Some phrases of His Holiness Pope Benedict XVI draw out attention to the same theme: "These days, the correct formation of believers' consciences is without a doubt one of the pastoral priorities"; and he adds: ""Spiritual direction" also contributes to forming consciences. Today there is a greater need than in the past for wise and holy "spiritual teachers": an important ecclesial service. This of course requires an inner vitality which must be implored as a gift from the Holy Spirit in intense and prolonged prayer and with a special training that must be acquired with care. Every priest moreover is called to administer divine mercy in the sacrament of Penance, through which he forgives sins in the name of Christ and helps the penitent to walk on the demanding path of holiness with an upright and informed conscience. To be able to carry out this indispensable ministry, every priest must tend to his own spiritual life and take care to keep himself pastorally and theologically up to date"[3]. It is in accord with this line of thought that that this aid is offered to priests as ministers of the Divine Mercy.

Any year dedicated to the memory of the *Curé of Ars* should leave an indelible mark on the life and ministry of priests. This is especially true of this year which recalls the 150th anniversary of his death (1859-

---

[2] SECOND VATICAN ECUMENICAL COUNCIL, Dogmatic Constitution *Lumen Gentium*, 9.

[3] BENEDICT XVI, *Message to His Eminence Cardinal James Stafford, Major Penitentiary, and to the participants of the course on the internal forum promoted by the Apostolic Penetentiary* (14 March 2009).

2009): "[a] Year, meant to deepen the commitment of all priests to interior renewal for the sake of a stronger and more incisive witness to the Gospel in today's world…"[4].

Such interior renewal should reach every aspect of priestly life and ministry and deeply permeate every aspect of their outlook, motivation and concrete behaviour. Contemporary circumstances demand witness to a priestly identity lived in joy and hope.

2. The ministry of the sacrament of reconciliation, which is closely connected with spiritual counselling or direction, tends towards recovery of the spiritual and apostolic objectives of both the minister and of the faithful, as a paschal return to the Father, in fidelity to his loving plan for "the fully-rounded development of the whole man and of all men"[5]. It implies personally undertaking anew, for the service of others, that journey of interpersonal relationship with God and with the brethren which is realized in contemplation, perfection, communion and mission. The practice of the sacrament of Penance in all its fullness, as well as spiritual direction or counselling, allows us to live more authentically in "joyful hope" (*Rom* 12:12). It allows us to respect and value human life in all its aspects, to rediscover the importance of the family and the guidance of young people, of the renaissance of priestly vocations and of an integrally lived priesthood, and of ecclesial and universal communion.

3. The relationship between reconciliation and spiritual direction is based on the urgency of love: "For the love of Christ impels us, once we have come to the conviction that one died for all; therefore, all have died. He indeed died for all, so that those who live might no longer live for themselves but for him who for their sake died and was raised" (*2 Cor.* 5:14-15). This presupposes a particular commitment since the followers of Christ truly "no longer live for themselves" (ibidem), but live in truth and charity.

All of the pastoral activity of St. Paul, together with its many difficulties, which he compares to the travail of childbirth, can be summarized in the urgency of "forming Christ" (*Gal* 4:19) in each and everyone of the

---

[4] BENEDICT XVI, *Letter Proclaiming a Year for Priests on the 150th Anniversary of the "Dies Natalis" of the Curé of Ars* (16 June 2009).

[5] PAUL VI, Encyclical Letter *Populorum Progressio* (26 March 1967), 42: *AAS* 59 (1987), 278.

faithful. St. Paul's objective was "to make everyone perfect in Christ" (*Col* 1:28) without exceptions or limits.

4. The ministry of reconciliation and the service of spiritual counsel and direction are contextualized by the universal call to holiness which is the perfection of Christian life and "the perfection of charity"[6]. Pastoral charity in the truth of priestly identity should cause the priest to direct all of his ministry and ministrations towards holiness thereby harmonizing the prophetic, liturgical and diaconal aspects of his ministry.[7]
An integral part of priestly ministry is the disposition to guide the baptized towards the perfection of charity.

5. The priest, as servant of the paschal mystery which he preaches and an instrument of Christ, celebrates and communicates, is called to be a confessor and spiritual director, beginning also from his own experience. He is minister of the Sacrament of Reconciliation and servant of spiritual direction just as he is, at the same time, a beneficiary of both of these means of sanctification in his own personal spiritual and apostolic renewal.

6. This present Aid hopes to afford a number of simple, factual, and inspiring examples drawn from numerous ecclesial documents (cited throughout) which may eventually be directly consulted. This is not intended as an exercise in casuistry but one of daily hope and encouragement.

---

[6] SECOND VATICAN ECUMENICAL COUNCIL, Dogmatic Constitution Lumen Gentium, 40.

[7] Cf. JOHN PAUL II, Apostolic Letter *Novo Millenio Ineunte* (6 January 2001), 30: *AAS* (2001), 287.

I. THE MINISTRY OF PENANCE AND RECONCILIATION LEADING TOWARDS CHRISTIAN HOLINESS

1. Contemporary importance, moment of grace

An urgent invitation

7. At the outset of the third millennium, John Paul II wrote: "I am also asking for renewed pastoral courage in ensuring that the day-to-day teaching of Christian communities persuasively and effectively presents the practice of the Sacrament of Reconciliation."[8] He also declared that it was his intention "to undertake a vigorous revitalization of the Sacrament of Reconciliation…[which] is a requirement of genuine charity and true pastoral justice" and recalled that the faithful, when they have the proper interior dispositions, have the right to receive personally the sacramental gift."[9]

8. The Church not only proclaims conversion and forgiveness but she is also the sign of reconciliation with God and man. The celebration of the Sacrament of Penance must be seen in the full context of ecclesial life and especially in the context of the paschal mystery celebrated in the Eucharist and in the context of a lived experience of Baptism, Confirmation and the command to love one another. Penance is always a joyful celebration of the Father's love who gives himself so as to destroy our sin when we recognise it in humility.

Christ's Mission operative in the Church

9. The Church's mission is a harmonious process of proclamation, celebration and of communicating forgiveness. This is especially true of the celebration of the Sacrament of Reconciliation which is a fruit and gift of the Risen Lord who is present in his Church: "Receive the Holy Spirit. If you forgive the sins of any, they are forgiven; if you retain the sins of any, they are retained" (*Jn* 20:22-23).

---

[8] JOHN PAUL II, Apostolic Letter *Novo Millenio Ineunte* (6 January 2001), 37, *l.c.*, 292.

[9] JOHN PAUL II, Apostolic Letter, given *Motu proprio, Misericordia Dei* on certain aspects of the celebration of the Sacrament of Penance (7 April 2002): AAS 94 (2002), 453.

The joy of forgiveness leads to an attitude of gratitude and generosity in the journey towards sanctification and in the mission. Those who have experienced forgiveness want others to experience this encounter with Christ the Good Shepherd. Thus, the ministers of the Sacrament of Penance who themselves experience the beauty of this sacramental encounter are always more disposed to offer this humble, arduous, patient and joyous service.

10. The concrete, joyful, trustworthy and committed practice of the Sacrament of Reconciliation is a clear indicator of the level of evangelization reached by the individual believer and by a particular community. The Sacrament of Penance is a eloquent sign of our desire for perfection, contemplation, fraternal communion and apostolic mission. "The practice of sacramental confession, in the context of the communion of saints, which serves in different ways to bring men closer to Christ, is an act of faith in the mystery of the Redemption and in its actualization in the Church."[10]

In the Sacrament of Penance, which is the fruit of the Lord's saving Blood, we experience that Christ who "was put to death for our sins and raised for our justification" (Rm 4:25). Thus, St. Paul affirms that "Christ reconciled us to himself and gave us the ministry of reconciliation" (2 Cor 5:18).

11. Reconciliation with God is inseparable from reconciliation with man (cf. Mt 5:24-25). This reconciliation is impossible without arriving at some form of purification of heart. All reconciliation comes from God because He forgives us our sins (cf. Ps 103:3). When we are forgiven by God, we learn better to forgive our neighbour and be reconciled with him.

Opening ourselves to love and reconciliation

12. Christ impels us to an ever more faithful love, to a more radical change (cf. Rev 2:16), so that Christian life may be imbued with sentiments of Christ (cf. Phil 2:5). Community celebration of the Sacrament of Penance, with personal confession of sins, can be of great assistance in living the ecclesial reality which is the communion of saints.

---

[10] JOHN PAUL II, Bull *Aperite Portas Redemptori* (6 January 1983), 6: *AAS* 75 (1983), 96.

13. The Christian tends towards full "reconciliation" following the "Our Father", the Beatitudes and the command to love. It is a journey of purification of sins and a journey of identification with Christ.

Today, this penitential journey is all the more important as a cornerstone and foundation for a society which lives communion. "The Church's wisdom has always pointed to the presence of original sin in social conditions and in the structure of society: 'Ignorance of the fact that man has a wounded nature inclined to evil gives rise to serious errors in the areas of education, politics, social action and morals.'"[11]

The witness and commitment of pastors

14. In every age of the Church's history, model confessors and spiritual directors can be found. *Reconciliatio et Paenitentia* (1984) mentions St John Nepomucene, St. John Mary Vianney, St. Joseph Cafasso and St. Leopold of Castelnuovo. In his discourse to the Apostolic Penitentiary,[12] Benedict XVI adds St. Pio of Pietrelcina.

Referring to these priestly models, John Paul II writes: "I also wish to pay homage to the innumerable host of holy and almost always anonymous confessors to whom is owed the salvation of so many souls who have been helped by them in conversion, in the struggle against sin and temptation, in spiritual progress and, in a word, in achieving holiness. I do not hesitate to say that even the great canonized saints are generally the fruit of those confessionals, and not only the saints but also the spiritual patrimony of the church and the flowering of a civilization permeated with the Christian spirit! Praise then to this silent army of our brothers who have served well and serve each day the cause of reconciliation through the ministry of sacramental penance."[13]

15. In many dioceses, and especially in minor basilicas, in cathedrals, in sanctuaries and in large urban parishes, the faithful have responded positively to the efforts of pastors to provide opportunities to approach

---

[11] BENEDICT XVI, Encyclical Letter *Caritas in Veritate* (29 June 2009), 34, quoting *The Catechism of the Catholic Church*, n.407.

[12] BENEDICT XVI, *Discourse to the confessors who serve in the four papal basilicas of Rome* (19 February 2007): *AAS* 99 (2007), 252.

[13] JOHN PAUL II, *Apostolic Exhortation Reconciliatio et Paenitentia* (2 December 1984), 29: *AAS* 77 (1985), 255-256.

the Sacrament of Penance. Since "through the Sacrament of Penance (the ministers) reconcile sinners with God and with the Church,"[14] this penitential celebration can also provide an opportunity for spiritual direction or counsel.

16. The priestly *munera* (duties) are closely joined to each other for the spiritual good of the faithful: "In the Church, and on behalf of the Church, priests are a sacramental representation of Jesus Christ – the head and shepherd – authoritatively proclaiming his word, repeating his acts of forgiveness and his offer of salvation – particularly in Baptism, Penance and the Eucharist, showing his loving concern to the point of a total gift of self for the flock, which they gather into unity and lead to the Father through Christ and in the Spirit"[15].

17. Priests are also invited to avail of this Sacrament: "The ministers of sacramental grace are intimately united to Christ our Saviour and Pastor through the fruitful reception of the sacraments, especially sacramental Penance, in which, prepared by the daily examination of conscience, the necessary conversion of heart and love for the Father of Mercy is greatly deepened"[16].

For this precise reason, *Pastores Dabo Vobis* invites priests to avail of this practice, which is a guarantee of their spiritual life: "I would like to make special mention of the Sacrament of Penance, of which priests are the ministers, but ought also to be its beneficiaries, becoming themselves witnesses of God's mercy toward sinners. Once again, I would like to set forth what I wrote in the exhortation *Reconciliatio et Paenitentia*: 'The priest's spiritual and pastoral life, like that of his brothers and sisters, lay and religious, depends, for its quality and fervour, on the frequent and conscientious personal practice of the Sacrament of Penance. The priest's celebration of the Eucharist and administration of the other sacraments, his pastoral zeal, his relationship with the faithful, his communion with his brother priests, his collaboration with his bishop, his life of prayer – in a word, the whole of his priestly existence, suffers an inexorable

---

[14] Second Vatican Ecumenical Council, Decree *Presbyterorum Ordinis*, 5.

[15] John Paul II, Post-Synodal Apostolic Exhortation *Pastores Dabo Vobis* (25 March 1992), 15: *AAS* 84 (1992), 680.

[16] *Ibid.*, 18.

decline if by negligence or for some other reason he fails to receive the Sacrament of Penance at regular intervals and in a spirit of genuine faith and devotion. If a priest were no longer to go to confession or properly confess his sins, his priestly being and his priestly action would feel its effects very soon, and this would also be noticed by the community of which he was the pastor'"[17]. But when I am conscious that God always forgives me, as Benedict XVI wrote, "by letting myself be forgiven, I learn to forgive others"[18].

18. Pastoral fruitfulness derives from the Mercy of God. Pastoral planning would hardly be efficacious were it to underestimate the importance of sacramental confession: "the greatest pastoral concern must be shown for this sacrament of the Church, the source of reconciliation, of peace and of joy for all of us who stand in need of the Lord's mercy and of healing from the wounds of sin... The Bishop will not fail to remind all those who by virtue of office are charged with the care of souls that they have the duty to provide the faithful with the opportunity of making an individual confession. He himself will make certain that the faithful are in fact being assisted in every way possible to make their confession... When one considers in the light of Tradition and the Church's Magisterium the close connection between the Sacrament of Reconciliation and participation in the Eucharist, one sees how necessary it is today to form the consciences of the faithful so that they may partake worthily and fruitfully of the Eucharistic Banquet, and approach it in a state of grace"[19].

The example of the Curé of Ars

19. The example of the *Curé of Ars* remains relevant for us today. The historical circumstances of his times were extremely difficult because of war, persecution, materialism and secularism. When he arrived into his parish, few approached the Sacrament of Penance. By the end of his life, huge numbers were coming to the sacrament even from other dioceses. For the *Curé of Ars*, the ministry of reconciliation was a "long martyrdom"

---

[17] *Ibid.*, 26: *l.c.* 699 quoting the Post-Synodal Apostolic Exhortation *Reconciliatio et Paenitentia* (2 December 1984), 31.

[18] BENEDICT XVI, *Letter to Seminarians* (18 October 2010), 3.

[19] JOHN PAUL II, Post-Synodal Apostolic Exhortation *Pastores Gregis* (16 October 2003), 39: *AAS* 96 (2004), 876-877.

which produced much abundant and healthy fruit. When confronted with the sinful condition, he used to remark, "what can we do, we cannot do anything except weep and pray". He lived "his life for poor sinners in hope of seeing them convert and weep [with repentance]"[20]. Frequent confession, even for those who are not in grave sin, has constantly been recommended by the Church as a means of progress in the Christian life[21].

20. In his letter to priests on Holy Thursday 1986, John Paul II, recalling the second centenary of the birth of the *Curé of Ars*, acknowledged that "it is undoubtedly his untiring devotion to the Sacrament of Reconciliation which revealed the principal charism of the *Curé of Ars* and it is rightly the reason for his renown. It is good that such an example should encourage us today to restore to the ministry of reconciliation all the attention which it deserves." The fact that great numbers of people "seem to stay away from confession completely, for various reasons, is a sign of the urgent need to develop a whole pastoral strategy of the Sacrament of Reconciliation. This will be done by constantly reminding Christians of the need to have a real relationship with God, to have a sense of sin when one is closed to God and to others, the need to be converted and, through the Church, to receive forgiveness as a free gift of God. They also need to be reminded of the conditions that enable the sacrament to be celebrated well, and in this regard to overcome prejudices, baseless fears and routine. Such a situation, at the same time, requires that we ourselves should remain greatly available for this ministry of forgiveness; ready to devote to it the necessary time and care, and I would even say giving it priority over other activities. The faithful will then realize the value that we attach to it, as did the *Curé of Ars*"[22].

The ministry of mercy

21. The ministry of reconciliation, when exercised with great generosity, will contribute to deepening the meaning of God's love, to recovering a sense of sin and of the imperfections which are obstacles to true love. Loss of a sense of sin disrupts the inner balance of our hearts and

---

[20] BLESSED JOHN XXIII, Encyclical Letter *Sacerdotii Nostri Primordia* (1 August 1959), 85, 88, 90: *AAS* 51 (1959), 573-574.

[21] Cf. *ibid.*, 95: *l.c.*, 574-575.

[22] JOHN PAUL II, *Letter to priests on Holy Thursday* 1986, 7: *AAS* 78 (1986), 695.

generates contradiction and conflict in human society. Only the peace of an undivided heart can overcome war and tensions. "The truth is that the imbalances under which the modern world labours are linked with that more basic imbalance which is rooted in the heart of man. For in man himself many elements wrestle with one another"[23].

22. The service of reconciliation, authentically exercised, will invite us to live in harmony with the heart of Christ. This is a pastoral "priority" since it requires living the charity of the Good Shepherd, living "his love of the Father in the Holy Spirit, his love for mankind even to the point of giving up his life as a victim for them."[24] In order to turn to God, we have to invite people to acknowledge their own sins in the sure knowledge that "God is greater than our heart" (1 *Jn* 3:20). The paschal joy of conversion – which produced saints and missionaries in every age – derives from this.

23. This importance of the Sacrament of Reconciliation is also evident in the reality of the pilgrim Church which "embracing in its bosom sinners, [is] at the same time holy and always in need of being purified, [and] always follows the way of penance and renewal"[25]. For this the Church looks to Mary who "shines forth on earth, until the day of the Lord shall come, as a sign of sure hope and solace to the people of God during its sojourn on earth"[26].

2. Fundamental approach

The nature of the Sacrament of Penance

24. The Sacrament of Forgiveness is an efficacious sign of the word, salvific action and presence of Christ the Redeemer. Through the sacrament, Christ prolongs his words of forgiveness in the words of the priest while, at the same time, transforming the attitude of the penitent who recognises that he is a sinner and asks forgiveness with the intent of expiation and a purpose of amendment. Actualized in the sacrament is the

---

[23] SECOND VATICAN ECUMENICAL COUNCIL, Pastoral Constitution *Gaudium et Spes*, 10.

[24] JOHN PAUL II, Post-Synodal Apostolic Exhortation *Pastores Dabo Vobis* (25 March 1992), 49: *l.c.*, 745.

[25] SECOND VATICAN ECUMENICAL COUNCIL, Dogmatic Constitution *Lumen Gentium*, 8.

[26] *Ibid.*, 68.

surprise of the prodigal son as his father forgives him and prepares a feast to celebrate the return of his beloved son (cf. *Lk* 15:22).

Paschal celebration, journey of conversion

25. The celebration of the sacrament is essentially liturgical, festive and joyful in that, guided by the Holy Spirit, it is oriented towards re-encounter with God and with the Good Shepherd. Jesus marked this forgiveness with festive and joyful tones (*Lk* 15:5-7; 9-10; 22-32). Frequent and regular celebration of the Sacrament of Penance is therefore understandable and desirable. Christ is readily encountered in this sacrament as he is encountered in the Eucharist, in the living word, in the community, in every person and also in the poverty of our own hearts.[27]

26. This sacrament also celebrates the call to conversion as a return to the Father (cf. Lk 15:18). It is called the Sacrament of Penance "since it consecrates the Christian sinner's personal and ecclesial steps of conversion, penance, and satisfaction"[28]. It is also called "the *Sacrament of Confession*, since the disclosure or confession of sins to a priest is an essential element of this sacrament. In a profound sense it is also a "confession" – acknowledgment and praise – of the holiness of God and of his mercy toward sinful man"[29]. It is also called the Sacrament of "forgiveness", "since by the priest's sacramental absolution God grants the penitent "pardon and peace", and the sacrament of "Reconciliation" since "it imparts to the sinner the love of God who reconciles"[30].

27. The sacramental celebration of "conversion" is closely bound to the challenge to respond to the love of God. For this reason, the call to conversion "is an essential component of the proclamation of the Kingdom."[31] It is in this way that the Christian is drawn [by] "the movement of a "contrite heart," (*Ps* 51:17) drawn and moved by grace (cf.

---

[27] "The Sacrament of Penance, which has such importance in the Christian life, renders present the redemptive efficacy of Christ's Paschal Mystery": BENEDICT XVI, *Discourse to the confessors who serve in the four papal basilicas of Rome* (19 February 2007): *l.c.*, 250.

[28] *Catechism of the Catholic Church*, n. 1423, b.

[29] *Ibid.*, n.1424.

[30] *Ibid.*; cf. 2 Cor 5:20; *Mt* 5:24.

[31] *Catechism of the Catholic Church*, n. 1427.

Jn 6:44; 12:32) to respond to the merciful love of God who loved us first (cf. 1*Jn* 4:10)"[32].

On the journey of holiness

28. This is a journey towards holiness which is called for and made possible by Baptism, the Eucharist, Confirmation and the Word of God. This is how that ministerial reality of grace operates and which St. Paul describes: "So we are ambassadors for Christ, God making his appeal through us. We beseech you on behalf of Christ: Be reconciled to God" (2 *Cor* 5:20). The special motivation of Paul's invitation is that God "made him sin who knew no sin, so that in him we might become the righteousness of God" (2 *Cor* 5:21). Thus, "now that you have been set free from sin and have become slaves of God, the return you get is sanctification and its end, eternal life" (*Rm* 6:22).

29. It is possible to experience this dynamic of the merciful forgiveness of God from childhood and even before First Holy Communion. "Innocent" children, moved by trust and filial joy, can find this experience[33]. For this reason and towards this end, such souls should be prepared with a truly adequate catechesis prior to receiving their First Holy Communion.

30. When we become involved with this evangelical dynamic, it becomes easy to understand the importance of confessing venial sins and imperfections as a conscious decision "to make progress in the life of the Spirit" and desire the transformation of our lives into an expression of divine mercy for others[34]. In this way, we harmonize ourselves with the sentiments of Christ who alone is the expiation of our sins (cf. *Rm* 3:25; 1 Jn 2:1-2)[35].

31. Once the priest is conscious of this reality of grace he cannot but encourage the faithful to approach the Sacrament of Penance. Thus, "when he celebrates the Sacrament of Penance, the priest is fulfilling the ministry of the Good Shepherd who seeks the lost sheep, of the Good

---

[32] *Ibid.*, n. 1428.

[33] Cf. JOHN PAUL II, *Address to Yugoslav seminarians* (26 April 1985).

[34] Cf. *Catechism of the Catholic Church*, n. 1458.

[35] *Ibid.*, n. 1460.

Samaritan who binds up wounds, of the Father who awaits the prodigal son and welcomes him on his return, and of the just and impartial judge whose judgement is both just and merciful. The priest is the sign and the instrument of God's merciful love for the sinner"[36]. "The Good Shepherd seeks out the lost sheep. When he finds him, he places him on those same shoulders which bore the wood of the Cross, and he carries him to eternal life"[37].

A mystery of grace

32. Respect for the "sacramental seal of confession" indicates that the penitential celebration of the sacrament is a reality of grace whose *iter* is already "traced out" in the Heart of Jesus and in deep friendship with him. Once again, the mystery and dignity of man are made manifest by the mystery of Christ.[38]

The effects of the grace of the sacrament are: reconciliation with God (restoration of peace and friendship with Him), reconciliation with the Church (reintegration with the communion of saints) and reconciliation with self (unification of one's own heart). As a consequence, the penitent "is reconciled with his brethren whom he has in some way offended and wounded. He is reconciled with the Church. He is reconciled with all creation"[39].

33. The dignity of the penitent emerges in the sacramental celebration in which he manifests his sincerity of his conversion and his sorrow. In effect, he is reintegrated "in the celebration of the sacrament by his acts which are completed by the words of absolution pronounced by the priest

---

[36] *Ibid.*, n. 1465.

[37] St. GREGORY NAZIANZEN, *Sermons*, 45.

[38] Cf. SECOND VATICAN ECUMENICAL COUNCIL, Pastoral Constitution *Gaudium et Spes*, 22. The ministry of reconciliation "must be protected in its sacrality both for the theological, juridical, psychological reasons on which I have already commented in previous discourses, but also because of the loving respect due intimate relationship between God and penitent by which it is characterized": John Paul II, *Discourse to the Apostolic Penitentiary* (12 March 1994), 3: *AAS* 87 (1995), 76; cf. *Catechism of the Catholic Church*, n. 1467.

[39] *Catechism of the Catholic Church*, n. 1469; cf. JOHN PAUL II, Post-Synodal Apostolic Exhortation *Reconciliatio et Paenitentia* (2 December 1984), 31, V: *l.c.*, 265.

in Christ's name[40]. Thus, we can say that "the Christian faithful, as he experiences the mercy of God in his life and proclaims it, celebrates with the priest the liturgy of the Church which is continually converted and renewed.[41]

34. The celebration of the sacrament actualizes a history of grace that derives from the Lord. "Down through history in the constant practice of the Church, the 'ministry of reconciliation' (2 *Cor* 5:18), conferred through the Sacraments of Baptism and Penance, has always been seen as an essential and highly esteemed pastoral duty of the priestly ministry, performed in obedience to the command of Jesus"[42].

35. It is a "sacramental" journey, an efficacious sign of grace, which forms part of the sacramentality of the Church. It is also the journey spelled out in the *Our Father* in which we ask for forgiveness while offering our pardon. This experience of reconciliation gives rise to a desire for peace for all mankind in the penitent's heart: "Christians long for the entire human family to call upon God as "Our Father!""[43].

3. Some Practical guidelines

The ministry of awakening the proper dispositions in the penitent

36. From the Church's earliest history, reconciliation and penance or "conversion" has assumed different forms of expressions and takes place at different times: the celebration of the Eucharist, special liturgical seasons (such as Lent), examination of conscience, filial prayer, almsgiving, sacrifice, etc. However, the really privileged moment for reconciliation and penance or conversion is with the celebration of the Sacrament of Penance or Reconciliation which, on the penitent's part, consists in contrition, confession, and satisfaction and which, on the priest's part, entails absolution and an invitation to greater openness to God's love.

---

[40] RITUALE ROMANUM – *Ordo Paenitentiae* (2 December 1973), Praenotanda 11: editio typica (1974)., pp. 15-16.

[41] *Ibid.*

[42] JOHN PAUL II, Apostolic Letter, given *Motu proprio, Misericordia Dei* (7 April 2002): *l.c.*, 452.

[43] BENEDICT XVI, Encyclical Letter *Caritas in Veritate* (29 June 2009), 79.

37. The clear, simple and integral confession of one's own sins restores communion with God and with one's neighbours, especially in the ecclesial community. "Conversion" as a return to following God's will, implies sincere repentance on the part of the penitent and thus an acknowledgement and disposition to amend one's own life. Accordingly, one's life is reoriented on the journey of love towards God and one's neighbour.

38. The penitent, in the presence of the Risen Christ in the sacrament (and in its minster), confesses his own sins, expresses his own sorrow and commits himself to amend his life. The grace of the Sacrament of Penance is the grace of forgiveness which reaches to the very roots of all sins committed after Baptism and heals our imperfections and deviations by imparting to the Christian the strength of "conversion" or the strength to be more open to the perfection of love.

39. The external gestures by which we give expression to an interior penitential disposition are multiple: prayer, almsgiving, sacrifice, the sanctification of liturgical times, etc. But "daily conversion and penance find their source and nourishment in the Eucharist"[44]. In the celebration of the Sacrament of Penance we experience that return journey described by Jesus in the parable of the prodigal son: "Only the heart of Christ who knows the depths of his Father's love could reveal to us the abyss of his mercy in so simple and beautiful a way"[45].

40. This grace of God, who took the initiative in loving us, permits the penitent to fulfil these gestures. The examination of conscience is conducted in the light of the love of God and of his Word. In acknowledging his own sins, the sinner assumes responsibility for them and, moved by grace, manifests his sorrow and abhorrence of sin especially before God who loves us and judges our actions with mercy. Therefore, the acknowledgement and integral confession of sins before the priest thanks to action of the Spirit of love, that goes well beyond the pain of contrition (out of love) or of attrition (out of fear of God's justice).

---

[44] *Catechism of the Catholic Church*, n. 1436.

[45] *Ibid.*, n. 1439.

The liturgical celebration

41. The celebration of the Sacrament of Reconciliation is a liturgical act. According to the Rite of Penance, it consists of a greeting and a blessing followed by the reading of the Word of God, an invitation to repentance, confession, counsel and exhortation, the imposition and acceptance of penance, absolution from sins, thanksgiving, a blessing and a dismissal[46]. The decorous and suitably positioned confessional "with a fixed grill between the penitent and the confessor in an open place so that the faithful who wish to can use them freely"[47] is of great use to both penitent and priest.

42. The ordinary form of confession, that is individual confession (even when preceded by a communal preparation) is an excellent opportunity to call people to a life of holiness and, consequently, for spiritual direction (with the same or another confessor). "Thanks then to its individual character, the first form of celebration makes it possible to link the Sacrament of Penance with something which is different but readily linked with it: I am referring to spiritual direction. So it is certainly true that personal decision and commitment are clearly signified and promoted in this first form"[48]. "When possible, it would be good that at particular times of the year, or whenever the opportunity presents itself, individual confession by a number of penitents should take place within penitential celebrations as provided for by the ritual, with due respect for the different liturgical traditions; here greater time can be devoted to the celebration of the word through the use of suitable readings"[49].

43. "In case of grave necessity recourse may be had to a *communal celebration of reconciliation with general confession and general absolution*". According to the norms of law, however, "for a member of the Christian faithful to receive validly sacramental absolution given to many at one time, it is required not only that the person be properly disposed, but also, at the same time, intend to confess within a suitable period of

[46] Benedict XVI, Post-Synodal Apostolic Exhortation *Verbum Domini*, 61.

[47] *Codex Iuris Canonici* (*CIC*), can. 964 § 2.

[48] John Paul II, Post-Synodal Apostolic Exhortation *Reconciliatio et Paenitentiae* (2 December 1984), 32: *l.c.*, 267-268.

[49] Benedict XVI, Post-Synodal Apostolic Exhortation *Verbum Domini*, 61.

time each grave sin which at the present time cannot be so confessed"[50]. The judgement as to whether the conditions required by the norm of law actually exist, "belongs to the diocesan bishop [who] can determine the cases of such necessity, attentive to the criteria agreed upon with the other members of the conference of bishops"[51].

Thus, "individual, integral confession and absolution remain the only ordinary way for the faithful to reconcile themselves with God and the Church, unless physical or moral impossibility excuses from this kind of confession... Personal confession is thus the form most expressive of reconciliation with God and with the Church"[52].

Practical norms given by the Church: an expression of pastoral charity

44. The Code of Canon Law contains practical norms for individual confession and communal celebrations,[53] as well as on the location and disposition of confessionals[54]. With regard to the minister of the sacrament, these norms reproduce norms drawn from the tested tradition of the Church and from her long experience. These norms would include matters such as the ordinary faculty to hear confessions and the faculty to absolve certain special cases[55]. It is therefore necessary to comply with everything disposed by the Church in regard to her moral teaching.[56] Confessors should always behave as just and merciful servants so that they may have "regard for the divine honour and [for] the salvation of souls"[57].

---

[50] *Catechism of the Catholic Church*, n. 1483; cf. *CIC*, can. 962 §1; *Codex Canonum Ecclessiarum Orientalium (CCEO)*, can. 721.

[51] Cf. CIC, can. 961; *CCEO*, can. 720.

[52] *Catechism of the Catholic Church*, n. 1484.

[53] *CIC*, cann. 959-963, *CCEO*, cann. 718-721.

[54] *Ibid.*, can. 964: "§1. The proper place to hear sacramental confessions is a church or oratory. §2. The conference of bishops is to establish norms regarding the confessional; it is to take care, however, that there are always confessionals with a fixed grate between the penitent and the confessor in an open place so that the faithful who wish to can use them freely. §3. Confessions are not to be heard outside a confessional without a just cause. Cf. *CCEO*, can. 736 §1.

[55] *CIC*, cann. 965-977; *CCEO*, cann. 722-730.

[56] *Ibid.*, can 978 § 2.

[57] *Ibid.*, can. 978 § 1; *CCEO*, can. 732 §2.

45. These norms both assist in the exercise of the due prudence "attentive to the condition and age of the penitent"[58] as well as affording practical guidance in determining "a suitable penance"[59]. It is precisely in this context of the mystery of divine grace and of the human heart that we can better understand the idea of sacramental "seal"[60].

Other norms are designed to assist the penitent in making a clear confession, such as the desire to express the number and kind of grave sins[61], at opportune times, or under particular circumstances (use of an interpreter), in full liberty, to an authorised priest of their own choice.[62]

46. The Rite of Penance also contains doctrinal and disciplinary norms on the Sacrament of Penance: preparation by the priest, welcoming, celebration of the sacrament in all its details. These guidelines aid the penitent in shaping his life according to the grace received in the sacrament. Thus, the communal celebration of the Rite of Penance, with individual absolution, is also a great help for individual confession, which is always the ordinary form of the celebration of the sacrament of Penance.

47. The Apostolic Letter, given *motu proprio, Misericordia Dei*, on some aspects of the celebration of the Sacrament of Penance of John Paul II, affords many practical norms to regulate the celebration of the sacrament in its diverse forms and with regard to its various aspects.

Orientation on the journey of holiness in harmony with the action of the Holy Spirit

48. In all of these various ways of celebrating the Sacrament of Penance, the most important thing is to assist the penitent in conforming himself to Christ. A simple and wise counsel can be an illumination for life or stir one to take seriously the process of contemplation and perfection under

---

[58] *Ibid.*, can. 979.

[59] CIC, can. 981. *CCEO*, can. 732 §1.

[60] Cf. *ibid.*, cann. 982-984. *CCEO*, cann. 731; 733-734.

[61] Cf. *CIC*, can. 988, §1: A member of the Christian faithful is obliged to confess in kind and number all grave sins committed after baptism and not yet remitted directly through the keys of the Church nor acknowledged in individual confession, of which the person has knowledge after diligent examination of conscience"

[62] Cf. *ibid.*, cann. 987-991; *CCEO*, can. 719.

the guidance of a good spiritual director (as we shall see in the second part of this document). The spiritual director is an instrument in God's hands, to help others discover what God desires for them in the present moment: his knowledge is not merely human knowledge. The homily at a communal celebration or a private counsel given in confession can have a life-long effect.

49. At every instant, attention must be paid to the process followed by the penitent. Sometimes, it may be necessary to help him arrive at a more radical conversion so that he can recover or re-enliven his fundamental option for the faith. At other times, the priest may have to assist the penitent in the normal process of sanctification which is one of integrated purification, illumination and union.

50. Frequent confession of venial sins or imperfections is a consequence of fidelity to Baptism and Confirmation, and expresses a sincere desire for perfection and return to the Father's plan so that Christ may truly live in us through a life of greater fidelity to the Holy Spirit. Hence, "in view of the fact that all the faithful are called to holiness, it is recommended that they confess venial sins also"[63].

Ministerial availability and fatherly welcome

51. Above all, prayer and penance are essential for the good of souls. It is thus, that genuine ministerial readiness and paternal acceptance will be possible.

52. Those, to whom the care of souls has been entrusted, "are obliged to make provision so that the confessions of the faithful entrusted to them are heard when they reasonably seek to be heard and that they have the opportunity to approach individual confession on days and at times established for their convenience"[64]. Where such happens, as we have already mentioned, there are often many positive results, and not only in some shrines but also in many parishes and churches.

---

[63] JOHN PAUL II Apostolic Letter, given *Motu proprio, Misericordia Dei* (7 April 2002), 3: *l.c.*, 456.

[64] *CIC*, can. 986. *CCEO*, can. 735.

53. An ever increasing ministerial readiness arouses the desire for Christian perfection. The priest's assistance, before or during confession, can bring him to a greater knowledge of himself and, in the light of faith, can arouse contrition and the intention of a permanent and personal conversion of life, as well as reparation, correction and amendment of life so as to overcome an insufficient response to the love of God.

54. The final part of the celebration of penance, recited after the absolution, strictly speaking, is the commendation. It contains a great wealth of spiritual and pastoral treasure. It should always be said given that it directs the heart of the penitent towards the passion of Christ, the merits of the Blessed Virgin Mary and of the Saints, and towards cooperation through subsequent good works.

55. By virtue of the fact that the priest acts in the name of Christ, the Good Shepherd, he has an impelling obligation to know the spiritual maladies of his flock and also to be close to the penitent. He has a duty of fidelity to the Church's Magisterium in matters pertaining to Christian morality and perfection, to living an authentic life of prayer, to be prudent in listening to penitents and in putting questions to them. He should also be available to those who reasonably request the sacrament and to follow the promptings of the Holy Spirit. This is a fraternal and paternal function of imitating the Good Shepherd and a pastoral priority. Christ, present in the celebration of the sacraments, is to be found in the hearts of penitents and calls his minister to prayer, study, the invocation of the Holy Spirit and paternal welcoming.

56. In this prospective of pastoral charity, we see that "an unwillingness to welcome the wounded sheep, and even to go out to them in order to bring them back into the fold, would be a sad sign of a lack of pastoral sensibility in those who, by priestly Ordination, must reflect the image of the Good Shepherd [...] It is particularly recommended that in places of worship confessors be visibly present [...] and that confessions be especially available before Masses, and even during Mass if there are other priests available, in order to meet the needs of the faithful[65]. In the event of

---

[65] JOHN PAUL II Apostolic Letter, given *Motu proprio, Misericordia Dei* (7 April 2002), 1b: *l.c.*, 455.

a concelebrated Mass, it is warmly recommended that some priests refrain from concelebrating so as to hear the confessions of the faithful[66].

57. The description of this ministry by the *Curé of Ars* highlights the aspects of welcome and readiness. Benedict XVI commenting on this writes: "We priests should feel that the following words, which he put on the lips of Christ, are meant for each of us personally: 'I will charge my ministers to proclaim to sinners that I am ever ready to welcome them, that my mercy is infinite.' From Saint John Mary Vianney we can learn to put our unfailing trust in the Sacrament of Penance, to set it once more at the centre of our pastoral concerns, and to take up the "dialogue of salvation" which it entails. The *Curé of Ars* dealt with different penitents in different ways[67]. In this context, we can understand his comments to a fellow priest: "I will tell you my recipe: I give sinners a small penance and the rest I do in their place"[68].

A renewed and up to date training for priests so as to be able to guide the faithful in different circumstances

58. One can learn from the *Curé of Ars* how to distinguish types of penitents in order to be able to assist them better in accordance to their dispositions. Although offering models of holiness to the more fervent, he exhorted all to steep themselves in the "torrent of divine mercy" thereby engendering the hope of emendation of life: "The good Lord knows everything. Even before you confess, he already knows that you will sin again, yet he still forgives you. How great is the love of our God: he *even forces himself to forget the future*, so that he can grant us his forgiveness!"[69]

This effort of pastoral charity "was undoubtedly for him the greatest of his mortifications, a form of martyrdom." Thus, "the Lord enabled him to reconcile great sinners who were repentant and also to guide to perfection

---

[66] Cf. Congregation for Divine Worship and the Discipline of the Sacraments, Reply *Quaenam sunt dispositiones* on norms relating to the celebration of the Sacrament of Penance (31 July 2001): Notitiae 37 (2001) 259-260 (EV 20 [2001] n. 1504).

[67] BENEDICT XVI, *Letter Proclaiming a Year for Priests on the 150th Anniversary of the "Dies Natalis" of the Curé of Ars* (16 June 2009).

[68] Cf. *Ibid.*

[69] *Ibid.*

souls thirsting for it"[70].

59. The confessor is a pastor, a father, a master, teacher, a spiritual judge and a physician who diagnoses and cures. "In hearing confessions the priest is to remember that he is equally a judge and a physician and has been established by God as a minister of divine justice and mercy, so that he has regard for the divine honour and the salvation of souls"[71].

60. Mary is Mother of Mercy because she is Mother of Christ the Priest who is the revealer of mercy. She, as no other, "obtained mercy in a particular and exceptional way... [she] is the one who has the deepest knowledge of the mystery of God's mercy" and thus a "particular fitness to reach all those who most easily accept the merciful love of a mother"[72]. The marian spirituality of each priest will allow his activities to be influenced by the maternal heart of Mary which is a reflection of the divine mercy.

New circumstances, new graces, new fervour of priests

61. We have to recognise the present difficulties facing the ministry of penance due to a certain loss of the sense of sin, a certain disaffection towards this sacrament, a certain blindness to the usefulness of the confession of sins and also the exhaustion suffered by many priests because of their manifold duties. However, confession is a spiritual rebirth transforming the sinner into a new creation and unites him with the friendship for Christ. Thus, it is a well-spring of joy for those who are servants of the Good Shepherd.

62. When the priest exercises this mystery, in a special way he enkindles his role as an instrument of a tremendous event of grace. In the light of faith, he can experience the actualisation of the loving mercy of the Father. The words and gestures of the priest are a means of realizing the real miracle of grace. While there are other ecclesial instruments which communicate the mercy of God (the Eucharist which is the greatest sign of his mercy), the celebration of the Sacrament of Penance accomplishes

---

[70] JOHN PAUL II, *Letter to priests on Holy Thursday* 1986, 7: *l.c.*, 695.

[71] *CIC*, can. 978 § 1. *CCEO*, can. 732 §2.

[72] JOHN PAUL II, Encyclical Letter *Dives in Misericordia*, 9; *l.c.*, 1208.

this in the most complete and eminent way[73]. It is a privileged means not only of encouraging those who receive forgiveness but also of generously following those who have embarked on the journey of identification with Christ. The journey of evangelical discipleship (on the part of the faithful as well as on the part of priests) requires this assistance so as to maintain its generous commitment.

63. This prospective of encouragement requires a greater attention to the training of the priest: "In this mysterious process of interior renewal the confessor is not a passive spectator, but *persona dramatis,* that is, an active instrument of divine mercy. Therefore, it is necessary that to a good spiritual and pastoral sensibility, he unites a serious theological, moral and pedagogical preparation that enables him to understand the life of the person. Furthermore, it is very useful for him to know the social, cultural and professional environment of those who approach the confessional in order to be able to offer appropriate advice and spiritual practices and orientations. To human wisdom, to theological preparation, therefore, one must add a profound spiritual disposition, nourished by prayerful contact with Christ, Master and Redeemer"[74]. The ongoing formation of clergy is of great assistance in this undertaking, for instance formation days for the clergy, special courses or programmes, such as those offered by the Apostolic Penitentiary.

---

[73] JOHN PAUL II, *Homily at Maribor (Slovenia)*, 19 May 1996.

[74] BENEDICT XVI, *Address to the Confessors who serve in the four papal basilicas of Rome* (19 February 2007); see also his *Discourse to participants in the course on the Internal Forum organized by the Tribunal of the Apostolic Penitentiary*, (7 March 2008). The allocutions of John Paul II and of Benedict XVI to the Apostolic Penitentiary offer an abundant catechesis on the celebration of the Sacrament of Penance while encouraging ministers to live it themselves and to assist the faithful in this experience of pardon and sanctification. In addition to the documents cited, the following can also be consulted: RITUALE ROMANUM – *Ordo penitentiae* (2 December 1973); JOHN PAUL II, Encyclical Letter *Dives in Misericordia* (30 November 1980); Post-Synodal Apostolic Exhortation *Reconciliatio et Paenitentia* (2 December 1984); Apostolic Letter given *Motu proprio, Misericordia Dei* on some aspects of the celebration of the Sacrament of Penance (7 April 2002); APOSTOLIC PENITENTIARY, *Il sacramento della penitenza nei Messaggi di Giovanni Paolo II alla Penitenzeria Apostolica 1981, 1989-2000* (13 June 2000); PONTIFICAL COUNCIL FOR THE FAMILY, *Vademecum per i confessori su alcuni temi di morale attenenti alla vita coniugale* (1997). The notes also cite the discourses of Benedict XVI to the Apostolic Penitentiary. See also: *CIC*, Book IV, Part I, title IV; *Catechism of the Catholic Church*, part II, article 4.

II. THE MINISTRY OF SPIRITUAL DIRECTION AS AN EXERCISE OF PASTORAL CHARITY

1. Contemporary importance, moment of grace

Historical and contemporary itinerary

64. Spiritual counselling has been practised from the earliest history of the Church down to our own times. It is sometimes referred to as spiritual direction or spiritual accompaniment. It is an ancient and tested practice which has produced fruits of holiness and evangelical readiness.

The Fathers, the Magisterium, numerous spiritual writers and the norms governing ecclesial life all speak of the need for spiritual direction, especially for those in training or formation, as well as for those in certain ecclesial conditions. There are certain moments in life which call for special discernment and for fraternal accompaniment. This stems from the logic of Christian life. "It is necessary to rediscover the great tradition of personal spiritual guidance which has always brought great and precious fruits to the Church's life"[75].

65. Our Lord was close to His disciples. Spiritual direction, under different names, has always existed in the Church. Initially, it was to be found in the monasteries of the East and West. From the Middle Ages, it was an essential part of the various schools of spirituality. As can be seen from the writings of St. Teresa of Avila, St. John of the Cross, St. Ignatius Loyola, St. Francis de Sales, St. Alphonsus Mary de Ligouri and from those of Cardinal Pierre de Bérulle, it had a much wider application in Christian life during the 16th and 17th centuries. While spiritual direction was always imparted by monks and priests, other members of the faithful (religious and lay) – Saint Catherine for example - have also given spiritual counsel. Ecclesiastical legislation has drawn on all of this experience and has applied it in the formulation of norms for formation for the priesthood and religious life. There are to be found also well formed lay people – both men and women – who offer this service of counsel along the journey of holiness.

---

[75] JOHN PAUL II, Post-Synodal Apostolic Exhortation *Pastores Dabo Vobis* (25 March 1992), 40: *l.c.*, 723

Priestly formation for spiritual accompaniment

66. Spiritual direction is a help on the journey of sanctification available to the faithful irrespective of their states of life. In present circumstances, while there is an increasing demand for spiritual direction on the part of the faithful, there is, likewise, an increasing need to better prepare priests to give spiritual direction. Such training would enable them to afford spiritual counsel with greater diligence, discernment and spiritual accompaniment. Where the practice of spiritual direction is available it issues in personal and community renewal, vocations, missionary spirit, and in the joy of hope.

67. The study of spiritual theology and the spiritual life become always more urgent during the period of preparation for the priesthood. In reality, spiritual direction is an integral aspect of the ministry of preaching and of reconciliation. The priest is called to guide souls along the path of identification with Christ and this also includes the path of contemplation. Spiritual direction as a discernment of the Spirit is part of the ministry. "While trying the spirits to see if they be of God, priests should uncover with a sense of faith, acknowledge with joy and foster with diligence the various humble and exalted charisms of the laity"[76].

68. From the first moment in the seminary, spiritual direction is an essential part of initial formation for the priesthood: "the students should be prepared by special religious formation, particularly through appropriate spiritual direction, to follow Christ the Redeemer with generosity of spirit and purity of heart"[77].

69. Spiritual direction is not simply a doctrinal consultation. Rather it concerns our relationship and intimate configuration with Christ. This is always Trinitarian: "The spiritual training should be closely connected with the doctrinal and pastoral, and, with the special help of the spiritual director, should be imparted in such a way that the students might learn to

---

[76] SECOND VATICAN ECUMENICAL COUNCIL, Decree *Presbyterorum Ordinis*, 9.

[77] SECOND VATICAN ECUMENICAL COUNCIL, Decree *Optatam Totius*, 3.

live in an intimate and unceasing union with the Father through His Son Jesus Christ in the Holy Spirit"[78].

Spiritual direction and priestly ministry

70. In describing the priestly *munera*, one must take account of their vital relationship with the spiritual life of the faithful: "You are ministers of the Eucharist and ministers of God's mercy in the Sacrament of Penance. It is you who bring comfort to people and guide them in difficult moments in their lives"[79].

Spiritual direction has always ascribed great importance to discernment of the Spirit leading to sanctification, the apostolic mission and communion in ecclesial life. The logic of the Spirit impels one to live in the truth and in goodness after the example of Christ. It is necessary to pray for His illumination and His strength in order to discern how to be faithful to His directives.

71. It can be said that attention to the spiritual life of the faithful, guiding them on the way of contemplation and perfection, and in assisting them in their vocational discernment, is a real pastoral priority: "From this point of view, the pastoral work of promoting vocations to the priesthood will also be able to find expression in a firm and encouraging invitation to spiritual direction. ... Priests, for their part, should be the first to devote time and energies to this work of education and personal spiritual guidance: They will never regret having neglected or put in second place so many other things which are themselves good and useful, if this proved necessary for them to be faithful to their ministry as co-operators of the Spirit in enlightening and guiding those who have been called"[80].

72. The pastoral care of young people, especially in assisting them to discern their proper vocation, also includes spiritual direction and counsel: "As Pope Paul VI wrote before his election to the pontificate: 'Spiritual direction has a wonderful purpose. We could say it is indispensable for the moral and spiritual education of young people who want to find what their

---

[78] *Ibid.*, 8.

[79] JOHN PAUL II, Post-Synodal Apostolic Exhortation *Pastores Dabo Vobis* (25 March 1992), 4: *l.c.*, 663.

[80] *Ibid.*, 40: *l.c.*, 724-725.

vocation in life is and follow it wherever it may lead, with utter loyalty. It retains its beneficial effect at all stages of life, when in the light and affection of a devout and prudent counsel one asks for a check on one's own right intention and for support in the generous fulfilment of one's own duties. It is a very delicate but immensely valuable psychological means. It is an educational and psychological art calling for deep responsibility in the one who practices it. Whereas for the one who receives it, it is a spiritual act of humility and trust"[81].

73. Spiritual direction is usually connected with the Sacrament of Penance, at least in the sense of a possible consequence, when the faithful request guidance on the path of holiness, including the specific journey of their personal vocation: "Along with the Sacrament of Reconciliation, the priest must also exercise the ministry of spiritual direction. The rediscovery and extension of this practice, also in moments outside of the administration of Penance, is greatly beneficial for the Church in these times. The generous and active attitude of priests in practising it also constitutes an important occasion for identifying and sustaining the vocations to the priesthood and to the various forms of consecrated life"[82].

Spiritual direction received by ordained ministers

74. Priests also need spiritual direction which is connected with Christ and animated by him: "In the fulfilment of their ministry with fidelity to the daily colloquy with Christ, a visit to and veneration of the Most Holy Eucharist, spiritual retreats and spiritual direction are of great worth"[83].

75. The reality of the ministry demands that the priest personally receive spiritual direction, seeking it out and following it with fidelity, so as to be better able to direct others: "In order to contribute to the improvement of their spirituality it is necessary that they themselves practice spiritual direction. By placing the formation of their souls in the hands of a wise fellow-member, they will enlighten the conscience, from the first steps in the ministry, and realise the importance of not walking alone along the

---

[81] *Ibid.*, 81; *l.c.*, 799-800.

[82] CONGREGATION FOR CLERGY, Directory on the ministry and life of priests *Dives Ecclesiae* (31 March 1994), 54: LEV 1994.

[83] SECOND VATICAN ECUMENICAL COUNCIL, Decree *Presbyterorum Ordinis,* 18.

paths of spiritual life and pastoral duties. In making use of this efficacious means of formation, so well-founded in the Church, priests will have full freedom in choosing the person who will guide them"[84].

76. Recourse to the counsel of our brothers and sisters is always necessary in resolving our personal and community questions. This is especially true when we turn to those who have the gift of counselling with greater intensity and to those, who, according to the grace of their state of life, exercise this gift in the context of the mission given to them, remembering that the prime "counsellor" or "director" is always the Holy Spirit, to whom we should pray constantly and with faith and trust.

2. Fundamental approach

Theological nature and basis

77. The Christian life is a "journey." It is a living in the Spirit (cf. *Gal* 5: 25) in harmony, relation, imitation and configuration to Christ by sharing in his divine sonship. Thus, all who are guided by the Spirit of God are sons of God (cf. *Rm* 8:14). Spiritual direction assists us to distinguish the spirit of truth from the spirit of error (cf. 1 Jn 4:6) and to clothe ourselves in the new man created in true holiness according to the justice of God (cf. *Eph* 4:24). Spiritual direction is of special assistance in discerning the *path of holiness and perfection.*

The basis for this practice of accompaniment or "spiritual direction" is the fact that the Church is a communion, the Mystical Body of Christ, a family of brothers and sisters helping each other according to the charisms each has received. The Church is a complex of various "mediations" which correspond to diverse ministries, vocations and charisms. We all have need of each other and especially in the field of spiritual counsel. This involves seeking out and accepting a counsel that comes from the Holy Spirit through our brothers and sisters.

We have all received the gifts of the Holy Spirit in Baptism and Confirmation. Among these gifts that of "counsel" is particularly significant. The experience of the Church shows that some people are favoured with this gift to a high degree and are called to serve others by

---

[84] CONGREGATION FOR CLERGY, Directory on the ministry and life of priests *Dives Ecclesiae* (31 March 1994), 54: LEV 1994.

using the gift they have received. Sometimes, spiritual direction can be exercised as an official office which has been entrusted by ecclesiastical authority or by the ecclesial community in which a person lives.

Specific objective

78. The principal objective of spiritual direction is therefore to discern the signs of God's will for our journey of vocation, prayer, perfection, for our daily life, and for our fraternal mission. Normally, we speak of discerning the illumination or promptings of the Spirit. Sometimes this discernment can be very urgent. It is always necessary to take account of the "charism" proper to personal vocation, or to the community in which the person seeking or receiving counsel resides.

79. In seeking to discern the signs of God's will, with the assistance of fraternal counsel, such consultation sometimes includes themes related to the moral life or to the practice of the virtues, and also presenting confidentially the situation which one wishes to clarify. However, a lack of a true desire for holiness will mean that spiritual direction has lost its objective. The objective of spiritual direction inheres in the process of faith, hope and charity (as configuration with the values, standards and outlook of Christ): It should always be guided by the signs of God's will for the charisms which we have received. The person being directed must always own his own responsibilities and initiatives.

80. Seeking moral guidance, disclosing one's problems in confidence, exercising the means of salvation must all be seen as part of seeking God's will. Without a sincere desire for holiness spiritual direction would never have a specific objective or purpose in Christian life.

Dynamism and process

81. The process of spiritual direction requires us to know ourselves according to the light of the Gospel and therefore to trust in God. This is a journey into a personal relationship with Christ in which, together with him, we learn and practice humility, trust and self-giving, according to the new commandment of love.

Conscience can be formed by teaching the mind, illuminating the memory, strengthening the will, orientating our desires, and encouraging generous commitment to sanctification.

82. Spiritual direction is structured according to stages. While these are not strictly ordered, they do develop like concentric circles: guide to a knowledge of self, trust in the love of God, making a total gift of self; trust in the harmony of purification, illumination and union. This is a dynamic of life harmonized with participation in the life of the Trinity (cf. *Jn* 14:23; *Eph* 2:18) through configuration with Christ (standards, values, behaviour: faith, hope charity...) and under the action of the Holy Spirit accepted with fidelity and generosity.

All this is worked out in a series of fields or areas - relationship with God, work, social relationships, integrity of life - in which we seek to find the will of God through counsel and accompaniment: prayer-journey, vocational discernment and fidelity, fidelity and self-giving in the way of perfection, harmonious living of fraternal ecclesial "communion" and commitment to mission. Spiritual accompaniment and counsel can also arrive at concrete measures to be applied in practice. In all of this process, it can never be forgotten that the true spiritual director is the Holy Spirit. The law protects all its duties and initiatives.

83. In the path of prayer (personal, communitarian, liturgical) we have to teach how to pray, paying special attention to the filial disposition of the Our Father which is one of humility, trust and love. Of much help for this pathway are the writings of the spiritual masters since they assist us in "opening our hearts and rejoicing in his presence" (*Curé of Ars*) in an exchange of glances, "I look at him, he looks at me" (the parishioner of Ars following the teachings of the *Curé*). It is thus that we accept the presence of Christ which is given to us and it is thus that we learn to make of our own presence a "resting with someone we know and love" (St. Teresa of Jesus). It is silence of adoration, of rapture and of self-giving as a "simple gaze of the heart" (St. Therese of Lisieux), but also speaking as Christ did in Gethsemane.

For all vocations and states of life

84. In accordance with the call of Jesus ("be you perfect then as your heavenly Father is perfect" *Mt* 5:48), the priest invites the faithful to undertake the "the path of that fullness of life proper to the children of God[85] so as to arrive at "a lived knowledge of Christ."[86] The demands of the Christian life (lay, religious and priestly) are incomprehensible without this "spiritual" life, or "life" according to the Spirit, which brings us to proclaim good news to the poor (cf. *Lk* 4:18).

85. On the journey of vocation, according to one's state of life special care is to be given, above all, to motivations and right intention, the freedom in choosing, formation in the realm of suitability and qualities.

Theological experts describe the spiritual director as one who guides in making concrete applications, inspires generosity in self-giving, and in proposing means of sanctification adapted to particular persons and circumstances, bearing in mind their specific vocations. Difficulties are confronted within the matrix of a serious attempt in the authentic following of Jesus.

86. Spiritual direction can be habitual or periodic or an occasional accompaniment *ad casum*. Initially, it can be more intense. It often happens that some of the faithful, in following their vocation, are encouraged to seek spiritual direction as a result of preaching, reading, retreats and prayer groups or, indeed, because they go to confession. A careful reading of the documents of the Magisterium can also arouse a need to seek out guidance so as to live more faithfully the Christian life. Such devotion to the spiritual life leads to greater social commitment: "Openness to God makes us open towards our brothers and sisters and towards an understanding of life as a joyful task to be accomplished in a spirit of solidarity"[87].

---

[85] JOHN PAUL II, Encyclical Letter *Veritatis Splendor* (6 August 1993), 115: *l.c.* 1224.

[86] *Ibid.*, 88: *l.c.* 1204.

[87] BENEDICT XVI, Encyclical Letter *Caritas in Veritate* (29 June 2009), 78.

3. Practical guidelines

Concrete itinerary of path of the spiritual life

87. Starting with this basic outline of the structure of spiritual direction and bearing in mind today's circumstances, the confluence of grace and contemporary sociological and cultural conditions, some practical guidelines can be indicated which are always open to new graces and new circumstances.

The application of spiritual direction must always take account of the specific ecclesial vocation of the person seeking direction or counsel. It must also look to their state of life, their particular charisms, and to the particular graces which have been given to them. Since a person is "unitary", it is necessary to know their particular circumstances: family, work, etc. When dealing with a specific charism or vocation, it is always helpful to note the various stages of its journey[88].

At all times, special attention must be afforded to special cases and to particular situations. These can include changes in the ecclesiastical state of life, the desire for greater perfection, scruples, and extraordinary phenomena.

88. The journey of spiritual direction can opportunely be embarked upon by a general revision of one's life. It is always useful to have a plan or some particular resolutions covering our relationship with God (liturgical and personal prayer), our fraternal relationships, the family, work, friendships, the specific virtues, our personal duties, the apostolate, and spiritual instruments. Such plans can also reflect our aspirations, the difficulties we encounter, and the desire to give ourselves increasingly to God. It is very useful to indicate precisely the spiritual method which you intend to adopt for the journey towards prayer, holiness (virtue), the duties of state, mortification and for the minor daily hardships of life[89].

---

[88] In the Codes of Canon Law spiritual direction is described for seminaries (*CIC*, can. 239; *CCEO*, cann. 337-339); in religious houses (*CIC*, can. 630; *CCEO*, cann. 433-475; 538, §3 - 539); and in secular institutes (*CIC*, can. 719) Further documentation can be consulted on spiritual direction for the priesthood, consecrated life, seminaries and novitiates in the final note of paragraph n.134 of this text.

[89] BENEDICT XVI, Encyclical Letter *Spe Salvi* (30 November 2007), 40: *AAS* 99 (2007), 1018.

89. There is an *initial moment* in which the subject is drawn towards dispositions of piety and perseverance in virtue, prayer, adhesion to the will of God, exercise of the apostolate, formation of character (memory, intelligence, affectivity, will), purification, formation to openness and a commitment to authenticity and renunciation of double standards. Thus, cases of spiritual aridness, inconstancy, superficial or transitory enthusiasm can be addressed. This is the opportune moment to root out and re-plant (cf. *Jer* 1:10) so as to identify and correctly orientate a dominant passion.

90. A second moment in spiritual direction known as the time of progress and advancement. At this stage in the process emphasis is placed on recollection, the interior life, increased humility and mortification, the deepening of the virtues, and the improvement in the life of prayer.

This stage leads to the stage of greater perfection in which prayer is more contemplative. Preferences are eradicated by distinguishing an "active" and "passive" aspect (or rather following faithfully the action of grace which is always surprising), so as to learn to overcome the dark night of the soul (or the dark night of faith). Deepening humility always results in increased charitable acts.

91. Each of the virtues requires a specific attention. It is along this path that we receive inspiration from the Holy Spirit and sense his promptings. This path leads to greater discernment and higher fidelity and generosity. Concrete cases of special graces or of spiritual or psychological weaknesses are confronted with special study, which should also involve the collaboration of others who are more expert and with a deep respect.

It is helpful to follow a plan that can be simply divided into principles, objectives and means. It is also useful to indicate where we want to go, where we are, where we have to go, the obstacles we can expect to encounter, and the means which we can employ.

92. The Eucharistic sacrifice, source and summit of the Christian life[90], integrity of life required in priests[91] and the faithful[92] all directly influence

---

[90] SECOND VATICAN ECUMENICAL COUNCIL, Dogmatic Constitution *Lumen Gentium*, 11.

[91] Cf. SECOND VATICAN ECUMENICAL COUNCIL, Decree *Presbyterorum Ordinis*, 14.

[92] Cf. JOHN PAUL II, Post-Synodal Apostolic Exhortation *Christifideles Laici* (30 December 1988), 59: *AAS* 81 (1989), 509.

the spiritual life. In addition to the principal means for the pursuit of the spiritual life (Eucharist, Word, prayer...) also important for their practical significance are *Lectio divina*, diverse forms of spiritual meditation, the assiduous practice of the Sacrament of Penance, spiritual reading, the examination of conscience (particular and general), spiritual exercises and retreats. Spiritual reading, drawn from the saints and from spiritual writers guides us on our journey of coming to know ourselves, on the journey of filial trust and of generous self-giving.

93. It is normal to encounter crises of growth or maturity while travelling along the Christian path. These can be felt to differing levels (purification, illumination, union). The "dark night" of faith can occur at various times but especially when the person comes closer to God. A certain "absence" of God or a profound "silence" can be experienced which is in fact a profound manifestation of God's presence and of His speaking with us. Spiritual direction is all the more necessary in these moments on condition that we follow the counsels given to us by the great saints and the spiritual masters.

The apostolate can also experience arid moments, conflict, misunderstandings, calumnies and persecution that can derive from error and even from good people (the persecution of the good). Spiritual counsel should help us to live the fertile mystery of the Cross by making of ourselves a special offering to Christ, our friend.

94. Special situations can also arise while travelling the Christian path. These can come about though the illumination or urging of the Holy Spirit and through a desire to make a greater commitment to the spiritual life or to the apostolate. However, there can be other moments which are illusory and deceptive and which derive from pride or fantasy. Those who travel the spiritual path can also experience discouragement, distrust, mediocrity, negligence or tepidness, excessive anxiety to be appreciated, false humility etc.

95. When extraordinary cases arise or extraordinary phenomena occur, these must be referred to the spiritual authors and to the great mystics. It has to be remembered that such phenomena can derive from natural sources, or from psychological and cultural sources as well as from formation and social contexts. The Church has established criteria to judge their

authenticity. These criteria are based on doctrinal content (illuminated by the Sacred Scriptures, the Sacred Tradition and the Magisterium) and on honesty of the persons involved (especially their sincerity, humility, charity and mental condition) and on the permanent fruits of holiness.

96. There are also illnesses and psychological weaknesses connected with the spiritual life. Usually, such take a spiritual character. They are generally rooted in some psychological cause such as lukewarmness deriving from the acceptance of habitual venial sin or imperfections, accompanied by an unwillingness to correct them. Mediocrity (superficiality, tiredness for work without the support of an interior spiritual life) may also produce such conditions. These weaknesses can also be connected to temperament: anxiety about perfection, erroneous fear of God, unfounded scruples, rigorism, lassitude, etc.

97. Those weaknesses or neuroses most connected with the spiritual life (such as hysteria) require professional attention (both spiritual and psychological). Usually, they manifest themselves in an excessive attention seeking or in deep dissatisfaction with the self (*hysterein*) which attempts to capture the attention and compassion of all. This often produces a climate of euphoric agitation into which the spiritual director can easily be drawn by believing himself to be protecting a victim or a special person. These manifestations have nothing to do with true contemplation and Christian mysticism which, while recognising human weakness, does not seek attention but expresses itself in humility, trust, and in an abnegation of self so as to serve others according to the will of God.

Discernment of the Holy Spirit in spiritual direction

98. It is easier to discern the *work of the Holy Spirit* in the life of each individual with the assistance of spiritual direction conducted in the light of a lived faith. This inevitably leads to prayer, humility, sacrifice, the ordinary life of Nazareth, service, and hope. We accomplish this in following the model St. Luke gives us of Jesus' life which was always guided by the Holy Spirit: towards the "desert" (*Lk* 4:1), the "poor" (*Lk* 4:18), paschal "joy" in the Spirit (*Lk* 10:21).

99. The works of the spirit of evil are accompanied by pride, independence, sadness, discouragement, jealousy, confusion, hatred, deception, disdain of others, and selfish preferences. Without spiritual direction it is very difficult to distinguish these areas especially in the absence of spiritual direction and taking into account temperament, culture, and natural qualities. The areas or themes which are to be discerned are those which belong to the path of vocation (as lived out in ordinary every day circumstances), contemplation, perfection, fraternal life and perfection. There are, however, personal and community situations which require special discernment; these would include a change in the state of life, new insights or impulses, structural changes, some weaknesses, and extraordinary phenomena.

100. Since the Spirit blows where he wills (*Jn* 3:28) it is not possible to formulate strict norms about discernment. However, the saints and the spiritual masters continually refer to certain constants or to signs of the actions of the Spirit of love who acts outside of human logic.

No spiritual situation can be well discerned without tranquillity of mind which is a gift of the Holy Spirit. It seeks out not one's own interest or to dominate others, but the best way of serving God and one's brothers and sisters. Spiritual counsel (in the context of discernment) operates with the guarantee of interior freedom which is not conditioned by selfish interests nor by the fashions of the moment.

Necessary for discernment are: prayer, humility, detachment from preferences, listening ability, study of the life and teaching of the saints, knowledge of the teaching of the Church, careful examination of personal interior inclinations, ability to change, and freedom of heart. In this way we can train a good conscience or form that charity which wells up from a pure heart, from a clear conscience and from a sincere faith (cf. 1 *Tim* 1:5).

Qualities of the spiritual director

101. Generally, it is required of the spiritual director that he should have a great welcoming disposition. He should be able to listen both patiently and responsibly. He should have a fatherly and friendly approach. He should be humble since this is a characteristic of all who offer the service of spiritual direction. He should avoid giving any impression of authoritarianism,

personalism, paternalism which induces affective dependence, haste or wasting time pursuing secondary questions. He should be prudent and discreet. He should know when to seek the advice of others with all the necessary reserve. All of these qualities and characteristics are drawn together when giving counsel. He should not overlook the importance of a healthy note of good humour which, if genuine, is always respectful and helps to resolve many artificial problems and to live more serenely.

102. In order to counsel spiritually, it is necessary to have a sufficient knowledge (theoretical and practical) of the spiritual life as well as experience of this and a good sense of responsibility and prudence. The qualities are harmonized in closeness, listening, hope, witness, integrity, in imparting a desire for holiness, firmness, clarity, truth, understanding, broadness or plurality of outlook, adaptability, perseverance on the path of holiness.

In general, the spiritual director (chosen, proposed or required) should be only one spiritual director so as to ensure continuity. Some of the saints consulted numerous spiritual directors and sometimes changed spiritual directors for the good of their spiritual lives. It should always be possible freely to change spiritual directors especially when there are serious reasons for suggesting that greater spiritual growth may require a change.

103. The spiritual director should know the person he is directing very well. This allows him to be able to search out the will of God with the person being directed so as to assist them on their spiritual journey and at times when special graces are poured out by God. Such diagnosis is dependent on the way we live, our qualities and defects, and the development of his personal spiritual life etc. The training should correspond to the grace given. The spiritual director is not making the spiritual journey; he follows it by assisting the person he is directing in their concrete life. The Holy Spirit is the one who directs souls and therefore the spiritual director should always support the action of the Holy Spirit.

The spiritual director should always have a profound respect for the conscience of the faithful. He should establish a relationship with the person being directed so that there is a spontaneous openness. He should always act with respect and delicacy. The exercise of the power of jurisdiction in the Church should always respect the reserve and the silence of the spiritual director.

104. The authority of the spiritual director is not one of jurisdiction, rather it is of counsel and guidance which, commands basic fidelity which can be a filial docility without, however, being paternalistic. This attitude of humility and of trust leads him to prayer and to the ability of not being discouraged when he is unable to see the fruits of his labours.

105. In the context of formation for the priesthood and the religious life, as well as in certain apostolic initiatives, it is usual to appoint some spiritual directors so as to ensure an adequate spiritual formation. This system should leave ample space for personal choice in choosing a spiritual director, especially in matters relating to conscience and to the Sacrament of Penance.

Qualities in the recipient of spiritual direction

106. The following qualities are required on the part of the persons receiving spiritual direction: openness, sincerity, authenticity, integrity, practice of the means of sanctification (liturgy, sacraments, prayer, sacrifice, and examination...). The frequency with which spiritual direction should be received depends on times and circumstances since there is no fixed rule about the matter. Initial stages of formation require a more frequent and assiduous use of spiritual direction. It is always better that spiritual direction is sought spontaneously rather than the subjects waiting to be called by their spiritual director.

107. The freedom of choice of director does not diminish the attitude of respect. Assistance is accepted in a spirit of faith. It has to be expressed with sobriety, orally or reading something previously written, taking one's own conscience into account and taking stock of one's particular location on the path traced out with regard to direction. Counsel can be sought on the virtues, defects, vocation, prayer, family life, fraternal life, proper duties (especially with regard to work), and on the apostolate. The basic disposition of the one receiving spiritual direction is that of someone who seeks to please God and be more faithful to His holy will.

108. The authenticity of the spiritual life will be seen by the harmony that exists between the counsels that have been sought and received, and a life that is lived in practical coherence to these. The particular examination of conscience is very useful in its own right, as is participation in spiritual retreats connected to spiritual direction.

109. The Christian must always enjoy complete freedom and responsibility in his life and action. It is the task of the spiritual director to assist the individual to choose and to choose responsibly that which he must do in the sight of God, with Christian maturity. The recipient of spiritual direction must freely and responsibly take up the spiritual counsel, and if he were to err he should not offload the responsibility onto the spiritual director.

Spiritual direction of the priest.

110. The ministry of the priest is linked to spiritual direction. However, he too has need of spiritual direction so as to be able to impart it better to others when asked so to do.

When a priest seeks spiritual direction, it is always necessary to bear in mind the fact that his charism and his particular spirituality has as its fulcrum "unity of life"[93] in the exercise of the sacred ministry. This "unity of life", according to the Second Vatican Council, is realised simply by priests in the concrete circumstances of their lives: "Priests can arrive at this only by following the example of Christ our Lord in their ministry. His food was to follow the will of him who had sent him to accomplish his work"[94]. These are gifts and charisms lived in strict relationship of dependence on the local bishop and his presbyterate of a local Church.

111. Above and beyond the daily celebration of the Eucharistic Sacrifice and the recitation of the Divine Office, a personal plan for the spiritual life of a priest could contain the following elements: dedicating some time each day to meditating on the Word of God, some time of spiritual reading, putting some time aside each day for a visit to the Blessed Sacrament or Eucharistic adoration, having fraternal gatherings every so often with other priests so as to be of mutual help to one another (coming together

---

[93] SECOND VATICAN ECUMENICAL COUNCIL, Decree *Presbyterorum Ordinis*, 14.
[94] *Ibid.*

for prayer, to share, prepare and collaborate upon homilies etc.), putting the Bishop's indications into practice insofar as it pertains to the direction of the Presbyterate (life plans, directories, ongoing formation, the pastoral work of priests etc.), daily reciting a marian prayer, found in the Holy Rosary, that one might remain faithful to these kinds of undertakings, making a daily particular and general examination of conscience[95].

112. In this ministry or service of spiritual direction, as in the Sacrament of Penance, the priest represents Christ the Good Shepherd, who is our guide, our brother, our father, our merciful physician. This service is closely connected with the ministry of preaching, and of guiding the community and by the witness of life.

113. Ministerial action is closely linked to spiritual direction. "Priests therefore, as educators in the faith, must see to it either by themselves or through others that the faithful are led individually in the Holy Spirit to a development of their own vocation according to the Gospel, to a sincere and practical charity, and to exercise that freedom with which Christ has made us free. Ceremonies however beautiful, or associations however flourishing, will be of little value if they are not directed toward the education of men to Christian maturity. In furthering this, priests should help men to see what is required and what is God's will in the important and unimportant events of life. Also, Christians should be taught that they live not only for themselves, but, according to the demands of the new law of charity; as every man has received grace, he must administer the same to others. In this way, all will discharge in a Christian manner their duties in the community of men"[96].

114. In fact, the one who appreciates spiritual direction and values it, not only recommends it in his ministry but also practices it personally.

If we do not lose sight of the objective of spiritual direction ways can always be found to ensure that spiritual direction is both given and received.

---

[95] Cf. CONGREGATION FOR THE CLERGY, Directory on the ministry and life of Priests *Dives Ecclesiae* (31 March 1994).

[96] SECOND VATICAN ECUMENICAL COUNCIL, Decree Presbyterorum Ordinis, 6.

115.   The invitation to practice spiritual direction should always be an important chapter in every pastoral plan. It should be a permanent invitation which ought always to have sanctification and mission for its objective. The faithful can be formed in this through preaching, catechesis, confession, the liturgical-sacramental life and especially of the Eucharist, Bible groups, prayer groups, the witness of the minister who himself asks for counsel in due time and in opportune circumstances. From some of these ministries or services, it is possible to pass to personal examination or to a personal encounter, to spiritual reading, to the spiritual exercises in personalized forms.

116. Spiritual direction, as a ministry, is often linked to the Sacrament of Penance in which the priest acts in the name of Christ, the Good Shepherd and shows himself as a father, a friend, a physician and as a spiritual guide. He is the servant of forgiveness and orients the journey of contemplation and of perfection, in full fidelity to the Magisterium and the spiritual tradition of the Church.

Spiritual direction in the consecrated life

117. Consecrated persons, according to their diverse ways, follow the same life of evangelic and apostolic radicalism by adding, "a special consecration"[97] through profession of "the evangelical counsels"[98]. Within consecrated life it is necessary to take account of the specific charism ("foundational charism") and of the special consecration that comes about (by profession), as well as the various forms of contemplative, evangelical, communitarian and missionary life, with their corresponding Constitutions, rules etc.

118. The journey to religious consecration provides several stages in immediate and long-term preparation, authentic deepening of a vocation with the support of evangelical convictions and motives (which dissipate identity issues), freedom of decision, so as to arrive at true worthiness and readiness for ordination or profession.

---

[97] JOHN PAUL II, Post-Synodal Apostolic Exhortation *Vita Consecrata* (25 March 1996), 2: *AAS* 88 (1996), 378.

[98] *Ibid.*, 30, *l.c.* 403.

119. There exist specific problems that can be considered as problems merely of "growth" or "maturity" if the consecrated person devotes an assiduous attention to spiritual direction: problems of physical or moral solitude, failures, affective immaturity, sincere friendships, interior freedom in fidelity to obedience, peacefully assuming celibacy as a sign of Christ the Spouse for his Spouse which is the Church, etc.

120. Spiritual direction of consecrated persons is marked by certain distinctive aspects in addition to those already mentioned with regard to the "vita apostolica." Apostleship, fraternal life, and mission are encouraged by a particular charism. This occurs in the context of a history of grace and of religious profession or special commitment to becoming witnesses in the world to a chaste Christ who was poor and obedient[99] and to being the "living memory of Christ's life and activity"[100].

This direction of the person belonging to the consecrated life presupposes a particular journey of contemplation, perfection, communion (common life) and mission which form part of the sacramentality of the Church as mystery, communion and mission. It is therefore necessary to receive and live out the gift since it involves "following Christ more closely… holding to the perfection of charity in service of the Kingdom"[101], tending towards a complete personal and spousal love which makes it possible "to be able to be "more deeply" present, in the heart of Christ, to one's contemporaries"[102].

121. Those priests who are invited to afford this service of spiritual direction will know that "that all religious, both men and women, who certainly have a distinguished place in the house of the Lord, deserve special care in their spiritual progress for the good of the whole Church"[103].

Spiritual direction for the laity

122. The universal call to holiness, in whatever Christian vocation, has no limits since it always involves a call to ultimate perfection: "Love

---

[99] *Ibid,.* 1: l.c., 377.

[100] *Ibid.,* 22: *l.c.,* 396.

[101] *Catechism of the Catholic Church,* n. 916; Cf. *CIC,* can 573.

[102] Cf. *Catechism of the Catholic Church,* n. 932.

[103] SECOND VATICAN ECUMENICAL COUNCIL, Decree *Presbyterorum Ordinis,* 6.

one another...be you perfect as your heavenly Father is perfect" (*Mt* 5:44,48). Spiritual direction intended for those of the faithful who are called to the sanctity in the lay state presupposes this vocation to Christian holiness distinguished, however, by its being an evangelical leaven in the world and which operates within its proper sphere and in communion with the Church[104]. The spiritual director should assist the lay faithful in their relationship with God (by making concrete their participation in the Holy Eucharist and prayer, in the examination of conscience in a manner that is in union with their lives), in forming conscience, in assisting with the sanctification of the family, work, social relationships, and taking part in public life. "Work done in this fashion becomes a prayer. Study done in this fashion is a prayer. Scientific research done in this fashion becomes a prayer. Everything converges to one solitary reality: all is prayer, everything can and should bring us to God, feeding our continuous relationship with Him, from sunrise to sunset. Every honest labour can be a prayer, and every work is prayer, it is an apostolate. In this manner the soul is strengthened in the unity of a simple but robust life[105].

As Benedict XVI reminded us, all the baptised are responsible for the proclamation of the Gospel: "The *laity* are called to exercise their own prophetic role, which derives directly from their Baptism, and to bear witness to the Gospel in daily life, wherever they find themselves"[106].

Spiritual direction or spiritual counsel for lay persons or seculars does not emphasize their failures or immaturity. Rather it is a fraternal assistance from the Director to work spiritually and apostolically according to the initiatives and responsibilities proper to the laity and in taking their place as authentic disciples of Christ in the world of human endeavour, of the family, of political and economic society etc. so as to sanctify the world from within.

123. Spiritual direction for the laity tends towards the path of holiness and mission without equivocation, given that they not only share in the priestly, prophetical or regal priesthood of Christ, as do all the baptized,[107] but also because they live this reality by a special grace which allows

---

[104] SECOND VATICAN ECUMENICAL COUNCIL, Dogmatic Constitution *Lumen Gentium,* 31.

[105] ST. JOSEMARÍA ESCRIVÁ, *È Gesù che Passa,* 10.

[106] BENEDICT XVI, Post-Synodal Apostolic Exhortation *Verbum Domini,* 94.

[107] *Ibid.*

them to be in the world and which gives to them a proper and absolutely necessary role in carrying out the Church's mission[108].

The laity "by their very vocation, seek the kingdom of God by engaging in temporal affairs and by ordering them according to the plan of God"[109]. They "generously dedicate themselves wholly to the advancement of the kingdom of God and to the reform and improvement of the temporal order in a Christian spirit"[110]. "It is their special task to order and to throw light upon these affairs in such a way that they may come into being and then continually increase according to Christ to the praise of the Creator and the Redeemer"[111].

Spiritual direction tends to make them participate in "the salvific mission of the Church"[112] thereby rendering them "present and operative in the temporal order"[113].

124. The assistance of spiritual counsel is necessary both in the interior life and in the various circumstances of life: social, family and professional engagement. It is above all necessary in those times of family and socio-political life in which it is necessary to give witness to basic or fundamental Christian values. At the busiest times of whatever apostolate one may be engaged in, it is always possible to find spiritual counsel where there is a desire to have it.

Harmonization of the various formative levels on the journey of spiritual direction

125. The person receiving spiritual direction is oriented towards configuration with Christ. Formation can be understood at different levels or dimensions: human, spiritual, intellectual, professional, pastoral. These various aspects of formation harmonize reciprocally with each other in view of ecclesial communion and mission. One always considers

---

[108] SECOND VATICAN ECUMENICAL COUNCIL, Decree *Apostolicam Actuositatem*, 1.

[109] Cf. SECOND VATICAN ECUMENICAL COUNCIL, Dogmatic Constitution *Lumen Gentium*, 31

[110] SECOND VATICAN ECUMENICAL COUNCIL, Decree *Apostolicam Actuositatem*, 4.

[111] SECOND VATICAN ECUMENICAL COUNCIL, Dogmatic Constitution *Lumen Gentium*, 31.

[112] *Ibid.* 33.

[113] SECOND VATICAN ECUMENICAL COUNCIL, Decree *Apostolicam Actuositatem*, 29; cf. JOHN PAUL II, Post-Synodal Apostolic Exhortation *Christifideles Laici* (30 December 1988), 7-8, 15, 25-27, 64: l.c., 403-405, 413-416, 436-442, 518-521.

the person as a member of a human and ecclesial community.

126. The human dimension or level must be taken well into account at both a personal and community phases given that the person must be correctly evaluated and know that he is loved and is able to love in the truth of grace. This presupposes a journey in freedom, an authentic set of values, motivations which are ordered towards love, dispositions to relate and for service. The person is constituted by relationship with the community.

Spiritual counsel is inspired by the ministry of Christ, in the light of which the human mystery is deciphered.[114] The person has to be trained to give and to give himself. Through this process, the person learns to listen, to be with others, to understand, to accompany, to dialogue, to cooperate, and to undertake sincere friendships.

In the Christian, human virtues are cultivated in the light of faith, hope and charity. This allows us to think, to evaluate and to love like Christ. The conciliar and post-conciliar texts of the Magisterium invite us to undertake this process of "human" formation which takes concrete form in a sensibility for justice and peace, harmony in diversity, capacity to take initiatives, admiration and openness to new values, constancy, fortitude, readiness for new initiatives, fraternity, sincerity, welcoming, listening, collaboration, attention to human relations and to good friendships[115].

127. The journey of spiritual direction, precisely because it is a journey of searching and of lived experience of the truth, of the good and of beauty, is an harmonious fabric woven of intelligence, affectivity, will, memory, and of things significant to us. Formation expresses itself in "in stability of mind, in an ability to make weighty decisions, and in a sound evaluation of men and events."[116]

It is a journey which harmonizes the fulfilment of duty, contemplative love, study and external action, in a necessary process for the "unity of life" in the apostolate.

---

[114] Cf. SECOND VATICAN ECUMENICAL COUNCIL, Pastoral Constitution *Gaudium et Spes*, 22.

[115] SECOND VATICAN ECUMENICAL COUNCIL, Decree *Presbyterorum Ordinis*, 3; *Ibid.*, Decree *Optatam Totius*, 11; JOHN PAUL II, Post-Synodal Apostolic Exhortation *Pastores Dabo Vobis* (25 March 1992), 43-44, 72: *l.c.*, 731-736; 783-787; CONGREGATION FOR CLERGY, Directory on the ministry and life of priests *Dives Ecclesiae* (31 March 1994), 76.

[116] SECOND VATICAN ECUMENICAL COUNCIL, Decree *Optatam Totius*, 11.

Spiritual direction helps us to know and overcome our own weaknesses, in the area of decision making, in memories, in sentiments, and in sociological, cultural and psychological conditioning.

128. In spiritual direction, one finds assistance to better organize the time of prayer, of family and community life, of commitment to children, of work and of rest, valuing interior and exterior silence, as well as discovering the positive value of difficulties and suffering.

Spiritual direction at this level answers three questions: who am I? (identity); with whom am I? (relations); and what purpose do I have? (mission). Under the influence of divine grace, I arrive at proper desires, principles, motivations, informed and correct values and dispositions, which derive from faith, hope and charity and the consequent moral virtues which is otherwise called life in Christ. The person is educated and formed to arrive at a self-realization by loving in the truth of giving oneself to God and one's neighbour.

In all of this process, account must be taken of the relationship between grace and nature (as with the relationship between faith and reason). This must be distinguished and harmonized since "Grace does not destroy nature, but perfects it"[117]. This is a principle of extreme importance when certain orientations and certain means have to be decided upon in matters touching psychology, cultural differences, and on the diversity of charisms which are found in different human conditions and especially in the content of faith.

129. It is necessary to find a unity of grace and nature. In this, preference must be given to the latter and seeing it as a participation in the new or divine life. "One aspect of the contemporary technological mindset is the tendency to consider the problems and emotions of the interior life from a purely psychological point of view, even to the point of neurological reductionism. In this way man's interiority is emptied of its meaning and gradually our awareness of the human soul's ontological depths, as probed by the saints, is lost. *The question of development is closely bound up with our understanding of the human soul*, insofar as we often reduce the self to the psyche and confuse the soul's health with emotional well-being. These over-simplifications stem from a profound failure to understand

---

[117] ST. THOMAS AQUINAS, *Summa Theologiae*, I, 1, 8 ad 2.

the spiritual life, and they obscure the fact that the development of individuals and peoples depends partly on the resolution of problems of a spiritual nature"[118].

130. Knowledge of temperament and character will help to ensure that aspirations to great things will not give rise to pride and independence (choleric temperament); that affability will not degenerate into vanity and superficiality (sanguine character); that the tendency to the interior life and solitude will not risk passivity and discouragement (melancholic temperament); that perseverance and equanimity will not become negligence (phlegmatic temperament).

It is at this human level, or dimension, that the question of "psychological assistance" arises. This form of direction "in certain cases and under precise conditions ... can be assisted, but not replaced, by forms of analysis or psychological help"[119]. In this regard, the documents of the Church which determine the opportunity and conditions under which these human instruments may be lawfully used[120].

131. As is evident, spiritual direction must give pride of place to the spiritual dimension because spiritual counsel is principally concerned with improving fidelity to our vocations, our relationship with God (prayer and contemplation), holiness and perfection, fraternity or ecclesial communion and our readiness for the apostolate.

In order to accomplish this, any programme for the spiritual life must be guided by a specific project (guidelines for the spiritual life), objectives to be accomplished at specific stages (purification, illumination, union) according to the maturity that has been reached by the recipient of direction and according to the corresponding methods.

---

[118] BENEDICT XVI, Encyclical Letter *Caritas in Veritate* (29 June 2009), 76.

[119] JOHN PAUL II, Post-Synodal Apostolic Exhortation *Pastores Dabo Vobis* (25 March 1992), 40: *l.c.*, 725.

[120] See in this regard: CONGREGATION FOR CATHOLIC EDUCATION, *A Guide to Formation in Priestly Celibacy* (11 April 1974); *"Guidelines for the Use of Psychology in the Admission and Formation of Candidates for the Priesthood"* (29 June 2008), *Instruction concerning the criteria for the discernment of vocations with regard to persons with homosexual tendencies in view of their admission to the Seminary and to Holy Orders* (4 November 2005): *AAS* 97 (2005), 1007 – 1013; *Directives on the formation of seminarians concerning problems related to marriage and the family* (19 March 1995).

132. The human-Christian and spiritual dimension must be nourished by study and reading. We could describe this as the *intellectual or doctrinal dimension* of spiritual direction. Fidelity to this journey is extremely difficult without a capacity for silent study and spiritual reading. The content of the faith must be studied especially in curricular instruction. However, intellectual formation (which is essential to the spiritual life) must continue to be broadened throughout life and be inspired by the saints, spiritual authors, and the spiritual classics.

Spiritual direction, in this intellectual or doctrinal dimension, could be valuable in filling the void encountered in the study of ecclesiastical material which should always be oriented towards the proclaimed, celebrated and lived mystery of Christ: "... towards the mystery of Christ. For it is this mystery which affects the whole history of the human race, continually influences the Church, and is especially at work in the priestly ministry"[121]. The Christological basis for the spiritual life is the most suitable basis for a successful preaching in guiding the faithful on the journey of contemplation, charity and in the apostolate.

Doctrinally oriented spiritual direction encourages a desire for individual and shared study as well as an assiduous reading of the great spiritual classics of the East and West.

133. Commitment to the apostolate is a necessary part of spiritual counsel and direction. Thus motivations, preferences, concrete reality ought be examined so that the person receiving direction becomes more disposed towards mission. Fidelity to the Holy Spirit infuses "them with a serene courage which impels them to pass on to others their experience of Jesus and the hope which motivates them"[122]. Only with this spiritual liberty, will the apostolate know how to overcome the personal and contextual difficulties of every age.

Spiritual direction, in this apostolic and pastoral dimension, includes giving witness, proclaiming Christ, celebrating the liturgy and offering service in the various areas of charity.

If spiritual direction is absent in the journey to perfection and evangelical generosity, it will be difficult for pastoral plans to include the

---

[121] SECOND VATICAN ECUMENICAL COUNCIL, Decree *Optatam Totius*, 14.

[122] JOHN PAUL II, Encyclical Letter *Redemptoris Missio* (7 December 1990), 24: *AAS* 83 (1991), 270-271.

principal orientation of pastoral activity itself which is that of bringing the faithful and communities to sanctity and identification with Christ (cf. 1 *Col* 1:28; Gal 4:19).

134. The path of Spiritual direction is to assist in making theological and pastoral formation relational. In whatever doctrinal or practical matter we always seek to live a personal encounter with Christ (cf. *Mk* 3:13-14), to live the apostolate (cf. *Mt* 4:22; Mk 10: 21-31.38), to live in communion with our neighbour (cf. *Lk* 10: 1; *Jn* 17: 21-23) so as to continue Christ's mission and share in it (*Jn* 20:21). The service of spiritual direction contributes to personal formation in order to build the communion of the Church[123].

---

[123] On spiritual direction, besides the documents already cited, see also the following: Second Vatican Ecumenical Council, Decree *Presbyterorum Ordinis*, 9, 18;, Decree *Optatam Totius* 3; 8; 19; John Paul II, Post-Synodal Apostolic Exhortation Pastores *Dabo Vobis* (25 March 1992), 40; 50; 81: *l.c.*, 725, 747, 799-800; Post-Synodal Apostolic Exhortation *Vita Consecrata* (25 March 1996), 21; 67; 46: *l.c.*, 394-395, 442-443, 418-420; CIC, cann. 239; 246; *CCEO* cann. 337-339, 346 §2; Congregation for Clergy, Directory on the ministry and life of Priests, *Dives Ecclesiae*, 39, 54, 85, 92; Congregation for Catholic Education, *Ratio Fundamentalis Institutionis Sacerdotalis* (19 March 1985), 44-59; *Circular Letter Concerning Some of the more Urgent Aspects of Spiritual Formation in Seminaries* (6 January 1980); *Directives concerning the preparation of Seminary Educators* (4 November 1993), 55; 61 (Spiritual director); Congregation for Institutes of Consecrated Life and Societies of Apostolic Life, Directives on Formation in Religious Institutes, *Potissimum Institutioni*, (2 February 1990), 13; 63: *AAS* 82 (1990), 479; 509-510; *Instruction Starting Afresh From Christ: A Renewed Commitment To Consecrated Life In The Third Millennium* (19 May 2002), 8; Congregation for the Evangelization of Peoples, *Pastoral Guide for Diocesan Priests in Churches dependent on the Congregation for the Evangelization of Peoples* (1 October 1989), 19-33 (spirituality and priestly life).

CONCLUSION:
"LET CHRIST BE FORMED IN YOU"
(*Gal* 4:19)

135. The priestly *munera* (duties), when exercised in the spirit of Christ, leaves a mark of "paschal joy"[124] and of "gladness of hope" in our hearts (cf. *Rm* 12:12). John Paul II recalled this when commemorating the bicentenary of the birth of the *Curé of Ars*: "Always be convinced of this, dear brother priests: this ministry of mercy is one of the most beautiful and most consoling. It enables you to enlighten consciences, to forgive them and to give them fresh vigour in the name of the Lord Jesus. It enables you to be for them a spiritual physician and counsellor; it remains "the irreplaceable manifestation and the test of the priestly ministry"[125].

136. The ministry of being a "spiritual counsellor and physician" is not just one of forgiving sins but of guiding and orienting the Christian life to correspond generously with God's loving plan for us. When the priest responds generously to this plan, that effective flowering of the graces which the Holy Spirit gives to his Church in every age becomes possible. The Second Vatican Council affirms as much when it states: "Hence, this holy council, to fulfil its pastoral desires of an internal renewal of the Church, of the spread of the Gospel in every land and of a dialogue with the world of today, strongly urges all priests that they strive always for that growth in holiness by which they will become consistently better instruments in the service of the whole People of God, using for this purpose those means which the Church has approved"[126].

The prophetic, liturgical and diaconal *munera*, exercised in this spirit, will ensure that the contents of the four constitutions of the Second Vatican Council will be applied in the Church which, being "sacrament" or transparent sign of Christ (*Lumen Gentium*) is the Church of the Word (*Dei Verbum*), of the Paschal Mystery (*Sacrosanctum Concilium*), present in the world and in solidarity with it (*Gaudium et Spes*), is *the mystery of communion for mission*.

---

[124] Second Vatican Ecumenical Council, Decree *Presbyterorum Ordinis*, 11.

[125] John Paul II, *Letter to Priests for Holy Thursday* 1986, 7: *l.c.*, 696.

[126] Second Vatican Ecumenical Council, Decree *Presbyterorum Ordinis*, 12.

As was the always the case in the implementation of the Councils, all of this implies a commitment of the baptized in their journey of holiness and their undertaking of the apostolate.

137. The pastoral care of holiness, which is proclaimed and realized in a special way in the *Sacrament of Reconcilliation and in spiritual direction*, and always in relation to the Holy Eucharist, is principally carried out by the priestly ministry, as the ministry that builds up unity (communion) at the heart of the human and ecclesial community.

138. The values of progress and technology need to be invested with a "soul" or a "spirituality", as Benedict XVI says: *"Development must include not just material growth but also spiritual growth*, since the human person is a "unity of body and soul", born of God's creative love and destined for eternal life. The human being develops when he grows in the spirit, when his soul comes to know itself and the truths that God has implanted deep within, when he enters into dialogue with himself and his Creator.... *There cannot be holistic development and universal common good unless people's spiritual and moral welfare is taken into account*, considered in their totality as body and soul"[127].

Spiritual direction of the baptized is an enthusing journey which impels the confessor or spiritual director to live joyfully his spiritual journey of giving to the Lord. "[This] requires new eyes and a new heart, capable of *rising above a materialistic vision of human events*, capable of glimpsing in development the "beyond" that technology cannot give. By following this path, it is possible to pursue the integral human development that takes its direction from the driving force of charity in truth"[128].

Thus, priests experience that "in their work they are never alone"[129]. They have been sent by the Risen Christ; they are accompanied by him and attended by him. His journey with them "which is only brought to fulfilment little by little through the collaboration of many ministries in building up the Body of Christ until it grows to the fullness of time"[130].

---

[127] BENEDICT XVI, Encyclical Letter Caritas in Veritate (29 June 2009), 76.

[128] *Ibid.*, 77.

[129] SECOND VATICAN ECUMENICAL COUNCIL, Decree *Presbyterorum Ordinis*, 22.

[130] *Ibid.*

139. The perennial reform of the Church's life needs an unequivocal note of hope. The growth of priestly and religious vocations and of ecclesial commitment on the part of the laity in the path of holiness and in the apostolate, requires a renewal of the ministry of penance and spiritual direction which should be exercised with well grounded enthusiasm and generous self-giving. This is the new Springtide which John Paul II hoped for: "Today, as never before, the Church has the opportunity of bringing the Gospel, by witness and word, to all people and nations. I see the dawning of a new missionary age, which will become a radiant day bearing an abundant harvest, if all Christians, and missionaries and young churches in particular, respond with generosity and holiness to the calls and challenges of our time"[131].

140. New situations and new graces nourish our hope for an apostolic fervour: "Like the apostles after Christ's Ascension, the Church must gather in the Upper Room 'together with Mary, the Mother of Jesus' (*Acts* 1:14), in order to pray for the Spirit and to gain strength and courage to carry out the missionary mandate. We too, like the apostles, need to be transformed and guided by the Spirit"[132]. The ministry of reconciliation and the service of spiritual direction are decided aids in this constant process of openness and fidelity to all the Church and, especially, of the ministerial priesthood's actualization of the activity of the Holy Spirit.

Vatican City, 9 March 2011
Ash Wednesday

MAURO Card. PIACENZA
Prefect

✠ CELSO MORGA IRUZUBIETA
Titular Archbishop of Alba marittima
Secretary

---

[131] John Paul II, Encyclical Letter *Redemptoris Missio* (7 December 1990), 92: *l.c.*, 339.
[132] *Ibid.*

APPENDIX I - EXAMINATION OF CONSCIENCE FOR PRIESTS

1. *"It is for their sakes that I sanctify myself, so that they, too, may be sanctified by the truth"* (*Jn* 17:19).

Do I really take holiness seriously in my priesthood? Am I convinced that the success of my priestly ministry comes from God and that, with the grace of the Holy Spirit, I have to identify myself with Christ and give my life for the salvation of the world?

2. *"This is my body"* (*Mt* 26:26).

Is the Holy Sacrifice of the Mass the centre of my spiritual life? Do I prepare well to celebrate Mass? Do I devoutly celebrate the Mass? Do I make an act of thanksgiving after Mass? Is the Mass the centre of my day in giving thanks and praise to God for his blessings? Do I have recourse to his goodness? Do I make reparation for my sins and for those of all mankind?

3. *"Zeal for your house consumes me"* (*Jn* 2:17).

Do I celebrate the Holy Sacrifice of the Mass according to the rites and rubrics established by the Church? Do I celebrate Holy Mass with a right intention and according to the approved liturgical books? Am I attentive to the sacred species conserved in the tabernacle and careful to renew it periodically? Do I pay due attention to the sacred vessels and ensure their conservation? Do I wear in a dignified fashion all of the sacred vestments prescribed by the Church? Am I conscious that I act *in persona Christi Capitis*?

4 *"Remain in my love"* (*Jn* 15:9).

Do I enjoy being in the presence of Christ in the Blessed Sacrament, in meditation and in silent adoration? Am I faithful to the daily visit to the Blessed Sacrament? Is the tabernacle my true treasure?

5. *"Explain the parable to us"* (*Mt* 13:36).

Do I carefully make a daily meditation and try to overcome all distractions which separate me from God? Do I seek illumination from the Lord whom I serve? Do I assiduously meditate on the Sacred Scriptures? Do I carefully say my habitual prayers?

6. It is necessary *"pray always and without tiring"* (*Lk* 18:1)

Do I celebrate the Liturgy of the Hours every day in an integral, dignified, attentive and devout manner? Am I faithful to my commitment to Christ in this important aspect of my ministry, praying in the name of the entire Church?

7. *"Come and follow me"* (*Mt* 19:21).

Is the Lord Jesus Christ the true love of my life? Do I joyfully observe my commitment to love before God in celibate continence? Am I given to impure thoughts, desires or actions? Do I indulge in improper conversation? Have I allowed myself to be in the proximate occasion of sin against chastity? Do I observe custody of the eyes? Have I been prudent in my dealings with the various categories of persons? Does my life represent for the faithful a true witness to the fact that holy purity is possible, fruitful and joyful?

8. *"Who are you?"* (*Jn* 1:20).

In my daily life, am I weak, lazy or indolent? Do my conversations conform to a sense of the natural and supernatural that a priest should have? Am I careful to ensure that there are no elements of vanity or superficiality in my life? Are all my actions consistent with my priestly state?

9. *The Son of Man has nowhere to lay his head* (*Mt* 8:20).

Do I love Christian poverty? Does my heart belong to God? Am I spiritually detached from everything else? Am I prepared to make sacrifices to better serve God? Am I prepared to give up my comforts, personal plans, and legitimate contacts, for God? Do I possess superfluous things? Do I make unnecessary expenditure or am I taken over by consumerism? Do I use my free time so as to be close to God remembering that I am always a priest –even in at these times?

10. *"You have hidden these things from the wise and learned and revealed them to mere children"* (*Mt* 11:25).

Am I guilty of the sins of pride: spiritual difficulties, susceptibility, irritation, unwillingness to forgive, tendencies to despondency, etc.? Do I ask God to give me the virtue of humility?

11. *"And there flowed out blood and water"* (*Jn* 19:34).

Am I convinced that when I act "in the person of Christ" that I am directly involved with the same Body of Christ, the Church? Can I sincerely say that I love the Church? Can I sincerely say that I strive with joy for her growth? Am I concerned for her interests, those of all her members and for the whole human race?

12. *"You are Peter"* (*Mt* 16:18).

Nihil sine Episcopo – nothing without the Bishop – was a saying of St Ignatius of Antioch. Are these words at the root of my ministry? Do I receive orders, counsels or correction from my Ordinary with docility? Do I pray often for the Holy Father? Am I in full communion with his teaching and intentions?

13. *"Love one another"* (*Jn* 13:34).

Have I been charitable in dealing with my brother priests? Does my egoism leave me indifferent to them? Have I criticised my brother priests? Have I supported those who are morally or physically ill? Am I committed to fraternal action so that no one is ever left alone? Do I treat all my brother priests and all of the laity with the charity and patience of Christ?

14. *"I am the way, the truth and the life"* (*Jn* 14:6).

Is my knowledge of the teaching of the Church as comprehensive as it should be? Do I assimilate and transmit her teachings? Am I conscious that to teach something contrary to the Magisterium, solemn or ordinary, is gravely abusive and causes damage to the faithful?

15. *"Go and sin no more"* (*Jn* 8:11).

Proclamation of the Word leads the faithful to the Sacraments. Do I regularly go to Confession? Do I frequently go to Confession in accordance with my state of life and because of the sacred things with which I am involved? Do I generously celebrate the Sacrament of Penance? Am I reasonably available to the faithful for spiritual direction and do I set particular times aside for this purpose? Do I carefully prepare to instruct in catechesis? Do I preach with zeal and with the love of God?

16. *"He called those to himself whom he willed and these went with him"* (*Mk* 3:13).

Am I careful to promote vocations to the priesthood and to the religious life? Do I promote a greater awareness of the universal call to holiness among the faithful? Do I encourage the faithful to pray for vocations and for the sanctification of the clergy?

17. *"The Man came not to be served but to serve"* (*Mt* 20:28).

Have I sought to devote myself to others and serve them every day according to the demands of the Gospel? Do I give witness to the Lord's charity by good works? Do I see the presence of Christ in the Cross and do I see in it the triumph of love? Is my daily activity marked by a spirit of service? Do I consider the exercise of authority as a form of service?

18. *"I thirst"* (*Jn* 19:28).

Have I prayed and generously made sacrifices for the good of the souls entrusted to my care by God? Do I discharge my pastoral duties? Am I solicitous for the Holy Souls?

19. *Behold your son. Behold your mother* (*Jn* 19: 26-27).

Do I entrust myself, full of hope, to the Blessed Virgin Mary, Mother of Priests, through love and to love all the more her son Jesus Christ? Do I practice marian devotion? Do I say the Rosary every day? Do I have recourse to her maternal intercession in my struggles with the devil, concupiscence, and the world?

20. *"Father, into your hands I commend my spirit"* (*Lk* 23:44).

Am I solicitous in assisting and in administering the sacraments to the dying? In my personal meditation, in catechesis and in my ordinary preaching, do I give consideration to the Church's teaching on the Last Things? Do I ask for the grace of perseverance? Do I ask the faithful to do likewise? Do I make frequent and devout suffrage for the souls of the faithful departed?

APPENDIX II - PRAYERS

ORATIO SACERDOTIS ANTEQUAM CONFESSIONES EXCIPIAT

Da mihi, Dómine, sédium tuárum assistrícem sapiéntiam, ut sciam iudicáre pópulum tuum in iustítia, et páuperes tuos in iudício. Fac me ita tractáre claves regni cælórum, ut nulli apériam, cui claudéndum sit, nulli claudam, cui aperiéndum. Sit inténtio mea pura, zelus meus sincérus, cáritas mea pátiens, labor meus fructuósus.

Sit in me lénitas non remíssa, aspéritas non sevéra; páuperem ne despíciam, díviti ne adúler. Fac me ad alliciéndos peccatóres suávem, ad interrogándos prudéntem, ad instruéndos perítum.

Tríbue, quæso, ad retrahéndos a malo sollértiam, ad confirmandos in bono sedulitátem, ad promovéndos ad melióra indústriam: in respónsis maturitátem, in consíliis rectitúdinem, in obscúris lumen, in impléxis sagacitátem, in árduis victóriam: inutílibus collóquiis ne detínear, pravis ne contáminer; álios salvem, me ipsum non perdam. Amen.

PRIEST'S PRAYER BEFORE HEARING CONFESSIONS

Grant to me, O Lord, that wisdom which stands beside Thy throne, that I may know how to judge Thy people with justice, and Thy poor ones with equity. Let me so use the keys of the Kingdom of heaven that I may open to no one upon whom they should shut, nor close them to any for whom they should open. May my intention be pure, my zeal sincere, my charity patient, my labour fruitful.

Let me be gentle without weakness, severe without harshness. Let me not disdain the poor; nor fawn the rich. Make me kind that I may attract sinners, prudent in questioning them, adroit in directing them.

Grant, I beseech Thee, skill to lead them back from sin, zeal in confirming them in good, diligence in elevating them to better things. Grant me good judgement in answering questions, correctness in counselling. Give me light when things are obscure, wisdom when they are entangled, victory when they are difficult. May I myself be not lost.

ORATIO SACERDOTIS POSTQUAM CONFESSIONES EXCEPERIT

Dómine Iesu Christe, dulcis amátor et sanctificátor animárum, purífica, óbsecro, per infusiónem Sancti Spíritus cor meum ab omni affectióne et cogitatióne vitiósa, et quidquid a me in meo múnere sive per neglegéntiam, sive per ignorántiam peccátum est, tua infiníta pietáte et misericórdia supplére dignéris. Comméndo in tuis amabilíssimis vulnéribus omens ánimas, quas ad pæniténtiam traxísti, et tuo pretiosíssimo Sánguine sanctificásti, ut eas a peccátis ómnibus custódias et in tuo timóre et amóre consérves, in virtútibus in dies magis promóveas, atque ad vitam perdúcas ætérnam: Qui cum Patre et Spíritu Sancto vivis et regnas in sǽcula sæculórum. Amen.

Dómine Iesu Christe, Fili Dei vivi, súscipe hoc obséquii mei ministérium in amóre illo superdigníssimo, quo beátam Maríam Magdalénam omnésque ad te confugiéntes peccatóres absolvísti, et quidquid in sacraménti huius administratione neglegénter minúsque digne perféci, tu per te supplére et satisfácere dignéris. Omnes et síngulos, qui mihi modo conféssi sunt, comméndo dulcíssimo Cordi tuo rogans, ut eósdem custódias et a recidíva præsérves atque post huius vitæ misériam mecum ad gáudia perdúcas ætérna. Amen.

PRIEST'S PRAYER AFTER HEARING CONFESSIONS

Lord Jesus Christ, sweet lover and sanctifier of souls, I pray you, through the infusion of the Holy Spirit, to purify my heart from every dissolute feeling or thought and to replace, through your infinite compassion and mercy, everything in my ministry which may be a cause of sin, due to my ignorance or neglect. I commend to your amiable wounds all the souls whom you have brought to repentance and sanctified through your precious blood so that you may guard them from every sin and keep in your love all who fear you, promote in them each day more virtues, and bring them to everlasting life. You who lives and reigns with the Father and the Holy Spirit for ever and ever. Amen

O Lord Jesus Christ, Son of the living God, receive this performance of my ministry with that surpassing love with which Thou didst absolve blessed Mary Magdalene and all sinners flying to Thee. Whatever in the administration of this Sacrament I may have performed negligently and unworthily, do Thou deign to supply and satisfy. I recommend to Thy most Sacred Heart all and each who have now confessed to me, asking Thee to guard them from relapse. After the misery of this life lead them with me into the joys of eternal life. Amen.

SUBJECT INDEX

Subject Index

Mission (*see* apostolate): 125-134.

Mission of Christ prolonged in the Church: 9-11.

Model Priests and confessors: 15-16.

Morality (*see* virtue): 61-63; 127-134.

Morality of marriage (*see* family, marriage).

Novices (*see* initial formation).

Our Father: 32-35.

Pardon: 21-27.

Paschal mystery (paschal celebration, journey to the resurrection): 9-11; 21-23.

Pastoral charity: 6244-47; 51-56.

Pastoral renewal: 7-8.

Pastoral work: 7-8; 14-18.

Pastoral work for vocations: 66-69.

Pastors (*see* Good Shepherd, pastoral charity): 14-18.

Peace (*see* reconciliation): 14-18.

Penance: 325-27; 41-43.

Penitent: 36-40.

Permanent formation: 66-69.

Personal and community celebration: 41-43.

Plan for priestly life: 117-121.

Prayer: 81-83.

Present situations: 10-30; 89-108.

Priest: 110-116.

Priestly life (cf. ministerial priesthood).

Priests and consecrated life: 117-121.

Priest as penitent and spiritual disciple: 14-18; 74-76; 110-116.

Proposals: 41-43; 51-57; 87-97.

Prudence: 44-47.

Psychology: 87-97; 125-134.

Qualities of the spiritual director: 101-105.

Qualities of spiritual disciple: 106-109.

Reconciliation: 12-18.

Radical, radicalism (*see* evangelical discipleship).

Redemption (*see* cross, paschal mystery, blood): 9-11; 64-65.

Reserve (secret): 32-35.

Resurrection (*see* paschal mystery).

Ritual of Penance: 41-47.

Sacrament of Penance:

- celebration: liturgy, acts of penance and ministry of the confessor: 41-43
- confession of sins and contrition, sorrow for sins: 36-40
- documents of the Church: 61-63
- expiation and proposals of amendment: 24; 36-40
- expression of pastoral charity: 44-47
- fidelity to disciplinary norms as an
- fruits of sanctity: 25-35
- importance and necessity: 7-23
- Institution: 9-11
- liberty in choice of confessor: 44-47
- minister: confessor, attitude, quality, welcome, invitation to holiness, duties; father; master, judge, physician, pastor: 36-36
- ministry of mercy: 21-23; 58-60
- mission of Christ prolonged in the Church: 7-8
- mystery of grace: 14-18
- nature and theological bases: 24
- paschal celebration: 15-27
- pastoral guidelines: 58-59
- paternal welcome: 51-57
- penitents: types, situations, qualities: 32-40; 44-47
- permanent formation of confessors and

69

penitents: 58-59.
- personal and community celebration: 41-47
- present difficulties: 36-40
- Sacrament of Penance and spiritual direction: 41-43; 70-76.
- See other aspects under various headings in this subject index.
- terminology of the sacrament: confession, penance, reconciliation: 25-27
- the priest as penitent: 14-18
- urgent invitation to ministerial readiness: 48-57
- witness and teaching of the Curé of Ars: 19-20; 51-59

Sacrifice: 36-40.
Saints and spiritual direction: 64-65.
Salvation, dialogue of salvation (*see* grace): 110-116.
Second Vatican Council (passim as cited in documents): Conclusion (synthesis of the Constitutions).
Seminary, seminarians (*see* initial formation): 66-69; 87-97; 125-134.
Service (*see* ministerial readiness).
Signs of the times: 98-100.
Sin, sense of sin: 25-31; 36-40.
Social doctrine: progress and development: 70-73; 135-140.
Sorrow for sins (*see* contrition).
Special cases in spiritual direction: 87-97.
Special examination: 106-109.
Spirit of evil: 78-80; 98-100.
Spiritual life: 81-83; 87-97.
Spiritual counsel (*see* spiritual direction): 70-73.

Spiritual direction:
- action of the Holy Spirit, personal and community discernment of the Spirit, prayer to the Holy Spirit: 66-73; 78-80; 98-100
- current issues and importance: 64-76
- documents of the Church: 125-134.
- free choice; levels and dimensions: human, spiritual, intellectual, apostolic: 125-134
- historical iter: 64-65
- in pastoral projects: 74-76
- journey of prayer and perfection: 81-83; 87-97; 125-134
- means of sanctity for the priest: 74-76
- ministry of the priest: 70-77; 110-116
- nature and theological foundation: 77
- objective: 78-80
- priest disciple: 74-76; 110-116
- seeking the will of God: 78-80; 98-100
- spiritual direction according to vocation: 84-86: priests: 110-121, consecrated life: 117-121, laity: 122-124
- terminology: spiritual direction, spiritual counsel, spiritual accompaniment: 77
- the disciple: qualities, docility, circumstances, free choice: 74-76; 110-116
- the spiritual director: qualities: 84-86
- training to give and receive spiritual direction: 66-69
- universal call to the holiness-perfection of charity: 81-82
- witness and teaching of the Curé of Ars: 74-76

Spiritual direction and confession: 41-43; 70-76.